From my Rousay Schoolbag

A history of the island's schools including reminiscences of schooldays by former pupils

Robert C. Marwick

Brinnoven

First published in 1995 by
Brinnoven, 9 Thomson Green,
Livingston, West Lothian, EH54 8TA

ISBN 1-899851-03-8

British Library Cataloguing in Publication Data.
A catalogue record for this book is available
from the British Library

Typeset in Adobe Utopia by
Willi Murray, 9 Thomson Green,
Livingston, West Lothian, EH54 8TA

Printed and bound by in Scotland by
The Orcadian Ltd, Victoria Street,
Kirkwall, Orkney, KW15 1DW

Contents

Tables

Illustrations

Photographs

The photographs are located between pages 48 and 49. The pupils and teachers shown in the group photographs (8 to 19) are listed on pages 83 to 85.

Preface

I first entered Wasbister Public School in Rousay in 1928 and moved on to Sourin a few years later. I soon became aware that across the road from each school stood a dwellinghouse called the Old School. I learned later that Frotoft also had an Old School, and for a long time I had known about the ruins of the Westside school which had served the people of Quandal prior to the clearances there in the middle of last century.

Were these the schools, I later wondered, which had been presided over by the stern, authoritarian schoolmasters I had heard old people talking about when I was a boy? Was it to these places that children of past generations had carried peats each day for the classroom fire? Who ran these old schools? Had there been even older schools, and, if so, where?

An interest in the past of my native island and a working life spent in schools combined to provide the incentive for tracking down the answers to my questions, and retirement provided me with the time that the search required. This small volume is the product of that labour.

I am indebted to Miss Alison Fraser, Archivist at the Orkney Library, for her help and advice, and to Mrs. Alison Mainland, Head Teacher of Rousay Community School, for giving me access to old logbooks. I also wish to thank Mrs. Sheena Marwick, the former Head Teacher at Rousay, for patiently answering my many queries about the new school. Mrs. Olive Kemp kindly provided the photograph of the Frotoft school. All the other photographs, and the information concerning them, were collected by Mr. Tom Gibson, and I am grateful to him for permission to use them.

I am especially grateful to all the former pupils who accepted my invitation to record memories of their schooldays in Rousay.

Robert C. Marwick,
Kilwinning, 1995.

To Rousay folk, where'er they be

'A School in every Parish' — John Knox

The Reformation reached Scotland in the middle of the 16th century and in 1560 John Knox and his colleagues produced their 'First Book of Discipline.' It contained a chapter on the provision of a national system of education in Scotland. An elementary school, teaching reading and elements of the catechism to 5-8 year olds, would be established in every parish. In towns of 'any repute' there would be grammar schools to teach Latin grammar to 8-12 year olds. At high schools in important towns selected 12-16 year olds would study Latin, Greek, logic, and rhetoric. Universities would offer 3-year Arts courses followed by one in medicine, law, or divinity lasting 5 years.

This ambitious scheme of the reformers came to naught because the Scottish Parliament did not accept it and also because the funding for it that Knox had in mind, namely, from confiscating the lands of the Old Faith, disappeared when the nobles, who had the necessary power, seized the lands and were not to be dispossessed. Knox's plan was nonetheless important as his vision of a school in every parish set the target for all those legislating for educational provision during the next 150 years.

The earliest attempt by the state to set up a school in every parish was an Act of the Privy Council of King James VI in 1616. The king's aim was 'to advance the true religion,' and he desired that all his subjects, especially the youth, 'be exercised and trayned up in civilitie, godliness, knowledge, and learning.' The king considered it 'necessary and expedient' to establish a school in every parish 'quhair convenient means may be had for entertayning a scoole'.

The 1616 Act stipulated that the young were to be taught reading and writing as well as being catechised and instructed in the grounds of religion. The cost of providing a suitable person to take charge of a school would fall on the parishioners. The Privy Council Act was not ratified by Parliament until 1633. Little was done, least of all in the Highlands and Islands, remote from the seat of power, to give effect to this well-meant piece of legislation largely because it contained no provision for its enforcement. Consequently, only thirteen years later, another Act had to be passed ordaining once more that a school be set up in every parish not already provided for, but this Act was no more effective than its predecessor.

Fifty years later, in 1696, came the Act for Settling Schools. It decreed that any parish which did not have a school should have one built and a schoolmaster appointed, all at the expense of the local landowners. Each landowner's share of the cost would be in proportion to his valued rent within the parish. The teacher's salary was fixed within the range of 100 to 200 merks (£5.55 to £11.10) per annum and payable half-yearly. A landowner was empowered to pass on half of his share of the cost to his tenants. A commodious building had to be provided for the school. In the event of disagreement among the landowners over sharing the costs, provision was made whereby the local Presbytery could ask the Commissioners of Supply to intervene in order to achieve compliance with the law.

The main weakness in this procedure stemmed from the fact that the Commissioners of Supply in many areas, including Orkney, were the very landowners on whom the financial burden of educational provision was to fall. Another weakness arose from the ministers' dependence on the landowners in their parishes for their stipends, and this made them disinclined to take any action that might incur the displeasure of their benefactors.

Because this legislation lacked effective measures for its enforcement it was inevitable that it would be disregarded in many parishes where lairds were unwilling to incur expenditure from which they could not see themselves deriving any benefits. Indeed, a short-sighted laird may well have reckoned that, by depriving his tenants of the means of advancing themselves through education, he was helping to ensure their greater readiness to comply with his wishes and to submit to his demands upon them.

'Society' Schools

Despite legislative efforts during the previous century for the wider provision of schools, the 18th century came in with very few parts of Scotland, apart from some towns, able to claim that their young people were receiving any schooling. This state of affairs, particularly as it affected the Highlands and Islands, exercised the minds of a 'few private gentlemen' in Edinburgh in 1701. These high-minded individuals were concerned about the ignorance and superstition which, they were convinced, were prevalent in these remote parts of their country and resolved that if nobody else would do anything to remedy matters then they would. They financed the setting up of a Charity School at Abertaf in Inverness but it met with so much opposition from the local population that it survived for only 18 months.

Despite this initial setback the 'few private gentlemen' persevered. They consulted widely, especially among influential friends and churchmen in Edinburgh. This resulted in the setting up of the Society in Scotland for Propagating Christian Knowledge (SSPCK). The aims of the Society were

> 'to further promote Christian Knowledge and the increase of piety and virtue within Scotland, especially in the Highlands and Islands, and remote corners thereof, where error, idolatry, superstition and ignorance do mostly abound, by reason of the largeness of parishes and the scarcity of schools, and for propagating the same in Popish and Infidel parts of the world.'

The Society was empowered under Letters Patent granted by Queen Anne to collect subscriptions and other funding and:

> 'therewith to erect and maintain schools to teach young people to read, especially the Holy Scriptures and other good and pious books; also to teach writing, arithmetic and such like degrees of knowledge, in the Highlands and remote corners of Scotland, and in other parts above mentioned, and to use such means of instructing the people in the Christian Reformed Protestant Religion as may be competent.'

With a large donation from the Church of Scotland, the Society's funds grew rapidly, and its first school was established in 1711 on the island of St. Kilda. The schoolmaster's salary was 300 merks (£16.60) and the community he served was expected to provide him with a house, a kailyard, and sufficient grazing for one cow. Shapinsay was the first place in Orkney to have a Society school but several other parishes including Harray, Rousay and Orphir were soon to be provided for.

In 1721 a petition had gone to the SSPCK from the Presbytery of the North Isles pleading Rousay's case for a school.

> 'The case of the island of Rousay is very lamentable, having no Schoolmaster, and the people for the most part both Ignorant and Barbarous, and the Presbytery entreats that a Charity school be settled there.'

Two years later a school was promised to the island which in turn promised that accommodation and a stack of peats would be provided for the schoolmaster. It was, however, to be another two years before the school was established on a small area of ground at Banks in Sourin. The building erected in 1725 was to house a school for the next 150 years and became a dwelling house in the 1870s when a new school was built across the road from it. The modern house which now occupies the site contains the shell of the 1725 building.

The North Isles Presbytery was asked to find a suitable person to take charge of the school in Sourin, and in due course the Rousay minister, Rev. Andrew Graham, reported that a David Marwick who had been doing some private teaching on the island was such a person. The Presbytery examined Marwick and found that he had 'sufficient knowledge of the principles of our holy Religion for that station and could read and write very well and had also competent knowledge in Arithmetick.' Having been tried and tested and found fit for his duties David Marwick became Rousay's first official schoolmaster. He was to remain in that post for the next 49 years.

When the SSPCK fixed a schoolmaster's salary at £16.60 in 1711 it decided that those in Orkney and Shetland should get by on half that amount until the Society's income increased. The records show that although the Society's income doubled between 1715 and 1732 the number of schools had more than quadrupled from 25 to 109 in the same period. So great was the demand for Society schools to be settled in the Highlands and Islands that in 1740 the amount the Society was prepared to pay towards a schoolmaster's salary was £3.33 per annum, and by the end of his 49 years' service David Marwick's salary had not risen beyond that amount.

Some schoolmasters benefited from a share of the Royal Bounty, an annual gift of £1,000 from the monarch, which was distributed to schoolmasters who were willing to act as catechists in their parishes. In some parishes the lairds contributed towards the teachers' salaries, and it may be that this was done in Rousay in order to augment the small amount paid to Marwick by the Society. However, lairds who agreed to help in this way frequently reneged on the agreement, leaving the Society in a difficult situation because it was reluctant to close a school as long as the teacher was prepared to struggle along on part salary.

It is worthy of note that in 1781 the SSPCK was running 180 schools in the Highlands and Islands, with 7,000 children being taught, on a total outlay of only £1,500 per annum. A president of the Society, commenting on that statistic 200 years later,

> 'feared that this achievement had only been possible by taking it for granted that the teachers engaged in this noble venture were prepared to live up to the Wordsworthian creed of plain living and high thinking.'

He went on to say that it must have meant very plain living indeed, for although in the early days the Society had paid their teachers £16.60 per year, many of them were 'content' to work for much less. Presumably the Sourin dominie was one who was 'content' to do so.

Parish ministers exercised a supervisory role over schools in their parishes on behalf of the Society and were encouraged to submit periodic reports on the work of the schools. In 1771 the Society engaged an ex-army officer to carry out an inspection of its schools in the Highlands and Islands. This task took him several months and although he did visit some schools in Orkney, the Rousay one was not included.

The SSPCK left a schoolmaster in no doubt about his priorities. He was required to instruct his scholars in

> 'the principles of the true Protestant Reformed religion; attentively to watch over their morals and to train them up in the social virtues; to worship God in the school morning and evening and to take care that the scholars attended church on Sunday; and to teach them to read and to speak the English tongue.'

This latter instruction reflected the strong anti-Roman Catholic feelings within the SSPCK in its early days. At that time the use of Gaelic was forbidden in Society schools but this policy did not survive for long. The teaching of Latin was also forbidden but there was a firm requirement for writing, arithmetic and church music to be taught.

The emphasis that was placed on religious instruction is clearly seen in Table 1. Compiled from reports sent in by the parish minister, it forms one of the few references to the Rousay school to be found in SSPCK records. It shows that all pupils were proficient in one or other of the subjects dealing with religion, and offers some proof that David Marwick was carrying out the Society's instructions on where the emphasis in his teaching was to lie. Arithmetic, by comparison, is seen to occupy a very lowly position. The highest number of children shown to be attending the school at that time was only 25, probably not more than half the number who were within reasonable walking distance of the school.

Table 1 — Proficiency in Learning

YEAR	1751	1755	1756	1757	1758	1759	1760
No. of Pupils	18	14	16	13	17	25	24
Bible	7	10	13	8	10	14	17
Testament	6	4	2	1	3	6	1
Proverbs	2	0	0	1	0	1	6
Catechism	3	0	1	3	4	4	0
Writing	5	4	8	5	7	8	13
Arithmetic	4	0	2	2	5	5	5
Music	0	0	0	0	0	0	0

It was SSPCK policy not to settle a school in any parish where a parochial school had not been provided by the local landowners as the Society had no desire to relieve the landowners of the responsibilities laid upon them under the 1696 Act.

However, the Society frequently departed from this policy, especially in places where the need for a school was great and the cost of providing one would not be high. Rousay was one such place where for half of the 18th century the Society maintained a school despite the absence of any moves by the landowners to carry out their obligations.

The Society's meagre annual payment to David Marwick ceased after 1774. This may have marked his retiral, or even his death, because by that time he was probably 70 years of age. Did the SSPCK decide to sever the Rousay connection in an attempt to force the landowners' hands over the provision of a parish school? The answer is not known, but after 1774 the Society's records contain no further reference to Rousay.

When its responsibilities for the running of schools were taken over by School Boards after the passing of the Education Act of 1872, the Society found itself with considerable funds on its hands. Two-thirds of its capital were transferred to the newly formed Highlands and Islands Education Trust and the rest was retained by the Society for its religious activities which continue to this day. Many Orcadian students have had cause to be grateful to the Highlands and Islands Trust whose bursaries financed their higher education in school, college, or university.

Sketch Map of Orkney

Rousay's Parish School

We have seen that the 1696 Act of the Scottish Parliament requiring landowners to establish schools in their parishes was widely disregarded in many parts of the country. In few areas was this more apparent than in Orkney. In 1775 Rev. John Scollay of Sanday reported to the SSPCK that nowhere in the North Isles of Orkney was there a parochial school. He pleaded with the Society not to withdraw its school in Sanday at that time in view of 'the difficulty of procuring parochial schools in an area so remote from the seat of justice,' thus identifying the basic weakness of the 1696 legislation.

It is not known when the Rousay lairds finally decided to honour their obligations. Undoubtedly, the withdrawal of the SSPCK from Sourin would have increased the pressure on them to do so. The existence of the Parish School is first mentioned in the minutes of the North Isles Presbytery where it is recorded that in 1805 William Leask was formally examined by Presbytery who granted him a certificate to enable him to draw the Parochial Schoolmaster's salary provided by the heritors (landowners) of Rousay. Ten years later the Presbytery was informed that Leask had died some months earlier and that his son Robert had been teaching the school since then.

The Parish School served the Quandal and Westness communities which had a population of 214 at the time of the 1841 census. This number included 41 children between the ages of 5 and 13. The building, the walls of which still stand, was centrally situated for the two communities it served, occupying a site on high ground above the old hill dyke. Although commanding a splendid view over Quandal and Eynhallow and across the sound to Costa Head, the location is one of the most exposed on the weather side of the island.

The schoolroom measured 20ft. by 12ft. with a 2-roomed house adjoining. Behind it lay a large walled area which was probably the schoolmaster's kailyard. Beyond that, a 3-acre stretch of ground was surrounded by a stone dyke. Near the house stood a small byre, now also in ruins, but identifiable by its dung hole set low in one wall. For a long time it had been stipulated that a rural schoolmaster should be provided with a house, a kailyard, and sufficient land on which to keep a cow. The Rousay provision corresponded exactly with these requirements.

The schoolmaster, Robert Yorston, wrote to the Presbytery in 1824 complaining about his salary and accommodation. The Rousay minister of the time, Mr. Paterson, was asked to investigate these complaints and to report back at the next meeting but the minutes make no mention of a report being made. The Presbytery required ministers to carry out annual inspections of the schools in their parishes and to submit reports of their findings. It appears that Mr. Paterson was rather lax in these matters for it is recorded that in 1832 his neglect of his school duties brought upon him "an expression of his colleagues' annoyance."

In the Statistical Account of 1845 it is reported that the Rousay schoolmaster's salary amounted to £26 per annum and his fees to £6. It was reckoned at that time that there were 41 children in the parish between the ages of 6 and 15 who were unable to read and 21 persons over 15 years in the same situation. The number of children in the parish (Rousay, Egilsay, Wyre, and Eynhallow) at that time was between 250 and 300 so the proportion unable to read was only about 1 in 7. This was a remarkably high rate of literacy at a time when school attendance was not compulsory. This level of literacy was common in Orkney and considerably higher than in most parts of Scotland. Few children stayed at school beyond the age of 13 and in the summer months attendance at school was always severely affected by the practice of keeping children at home to do herding and other tasks.

James Brotchie, a divinity student, took charge of the school in 1832 after satisfying the Presbytery regarding his moral character and his proficiency in 'the proper branches of education.' After five years in the post he left to become assistant minister in Westray. Brotchie was succeeded by George Robson who came from the Society school in Stenness. It is recorded that he had been elected at a meeting of the heritors and that the Presbytery 'examined him in English, Reading and Grammar, Arithmetic, Navigation, Latin, and Greek, and having found him qualified to teach all these Branches, confirmed his appointment to the office of Parochial Schoolmaster.' Robson, who was a native of Banff, came to Rousay in 1838 and a few years later married a local girl, Janet Murray. He stayed for sixteen years and was replaced by a Caithness man, Sinclair McKay. Like his predecessor, McKay married shortly after coming to the island, his wife being Mary Corsie from Skaill.

In 1833 the government had begun making grants available to assist with the cost of providing school buildings and the paying of teachers' salaries. These grants carried the right of government inspection and it is noted in the North Isles Presbytery minutes that in 1857 Dr. Woodford, Her Majesty's Inspector, inspected the parish school in Rousay. By 1862 the grants had been fixed at 12 shillings (60p) per pupil per year, 4 shillings being for satisfactory attendance and 8 shillings for reaching certain standards in the basic subjects of reading, writing, and arithmetic. There were 6 standards and no pupil could be presented twice in the same standard no matter how poor his/her previous performance had been. This forced teachers to give more attention than hitherto to the less able pupils in order to attract grant.

Table 2 — Number of Children Aged 5 to 13 Years in Quandal/Westness District

YEAR	1841	1851	1861	1871	1881
	41	33	16	14	12

The clearance of people from the main part of Quandal took place in the late 1840s and, as the Table 2 shows, resulted in the potential roll of the Parish School dropping from 41 to 33 between 1841 and 1851. It should be remembered that compulsory attendance was still more than twenty years away but as we have already seen, the level of literacy indicated that voluntary attendance reached a high level. In 1841 there were 41 children in the district and if a high proportion of them attended school, one wonders how they all managed to crowd into that small classroom. The number of children dropped by half during the 1850s when the larger holdings such as Skaill and Brough, lying nearer Westness, were absorbed into Westness Farm after the expiry of their leases. It was during that period also that those crofts which lay on the upper fringes of Quandal, such as Stourameadow and Flintersquoy, were cleared. The families remaining in the district after 1860 were mainly employed on Westness Farm.

Sinclair McKay was still presiding over the Westside school in 1861, but by 1871 he had been transferred to a new Parish School in Frotoft, built on the high ground above Tratland. This new school was taken over in 1873 by the Rousay School Board which was an elected body brought into being by the Education Act of 1872. There had been an earlier school in the Frotoft district. It was housed in a small building which lies a little way to the east of Hullion. Little is known of this school which must have been the only one available for the Frotoft children, the old Parish School in Quandal being too far away for them to walk to it. In March, 1867, *The Orcadian* carried a news item from Rousay reporting that the Subscription School at Frotoft had been examined. The teacher at that time was William McLellan. It is likely that many pupils from this school moved to the new Parish School above Tratland when it was opened, but the old school near Hullion may not have ceased operations entirely at that time. Shortly after the School Board took over the Parish School in 1873, it was reported that the majority of the pupils in Frotoft were attending another school in the district. When it eventually closed down the building became a dwellinghouse which fell into ruins after its last occupant died in 1960.

The former Parish School in its windblown position in the Westside became a dwellinghouse for the shepherd looking after the Westness flocks. The last shepherd to live there was Charlie Louttit who was killed in France in the First World War. The roof of Caithness slate was removed in 1921 to be used on the new house at Bigland.

The Assembly School

From its earliest days, the Church of Scotland has had a proud record of involvement in Scottish education. It was closely involved with the SSPCK and had contributed generously to its funds. Parish ministers had a supervisory role in the Society's schools, sending in periodic reports on them to the Society's headquarters in Edinburgh, and before government inspections were introduced, ministers carried out inspections of parish schools on behalf of the local presbytery.

The General Assembly of 1824 expressed concern over the lack of adequate schooling in many of its parishes. Some parishes still had no schools at all. Ministers pointed out that a single school in a parish that covered a large area—and there were many such parishes in rural Scotland—was, in many cases, outwith the reach of children from the remoter parts of the parish. Apart from its moral duty of encouraging the provision of education for all its people, the Church of Scotland saw schools as important centres of religious teaching. The Assembly decided to set up an Education Committee which it charged with the task of settling schools in places where the need was greatest, with the clearly expressed aim of making them 'essentially and effectively bible schools.' To finance the undertaking, the Assembly ordered a special collection to be taken up in every parish. The proceeds from half the parishes amounted to £5488 by 1826. The heritors were to provide the necessary land and buildings and the Committee would pay the schoolmasters at a rate of £20 - £25 per annum. A teacher would be at liberty to charge fees to augment his meagre salary. The Church trained its own teachers but by offering such low salaries, Assembly schools failed to attract quality teachers who could obtain higher rewards in Parish schools.

The curriculum in Assembly schools was fairly basic, consisting of reading, writing and arithmetic, and of course, religious instruction. Girls were given instruction in sewing and knitting.

By 1827 an Assembly school had been established at Sourin. The premises which had been provided for the SSPCK school a century earlier were pressed into use once more. The schoolmaster was William Smeaton who remained in post till 1843. He 'came out' at the Disruption and joined the Free Kirk, as did many other Assembly and Society teachers. Consequently, many of them, including Mr. Smeaton, were dismissed from their posts. He was succeeded by Thomas B. Reid, a Shapinsay man, who was not without his critics in Sourin. In September, 1851 the Assembly's Education Committee decided to dismiss him after receiving an unfavourable report from the parish minister. Later, the Committee had a change of mind and decided to retain him until the Secretary could visit Rousay and judge the situation for himself. Reid escaped dismissal at that time and continued to serve in Sourin until the School Board took over more than twenty years later.

The Free Kirk School

In 1843 a great many ministers and members of their congregations left the Church of Scotland and formed the Free Church. This breakaway, known as the Disruption, was brought about mainly through dissatisfaction with the practice of patronage, whereby the patron in a parish, usually the largest landowner, had the right to select the parish minister. The Rousay minister, Rev. George Ritchie, was one of those who 'came out' along with almost the whole of his congregation. Education throughout Scotland benefited greatly from this development because within a few years the Free Church had opened 500 new schools, many of them in districts where no schools had previously existed.

Only two years after it came into being, the Rousay Free Kirk, under Ritchie's leadership, was granted one acre of land on Falquoy in Wasbister on which to build a school. The land was gifted by George W. Searle who, along with a fellow landowner, the Earl of Zetland, also contributed £5 annually towards the teacher's salary. Shortly afterwards, the school and adjoining schoolhouse were built, and the first teacher, William Linklater, appointed.

Contributions from various sources helped to pay the teacher's salary. Besides the annual donation of £5 from the two landowners, there was also £5 from the Free Church's Education Fund. The Kirk records show that during the 1860s the average annual collection in the district for the Schoolmaster's Sustenation Fund amounted to £3.50. In addition, the teacher also had the benefit of fees that were levied but such was the poverty in many families that constant difficulty was experienced in collecting the fees. In 1860 the local Free Kirk decided to pay the fees owed by its members 'in order that the teacher, whose income is very inadequate, may not be put to any loss.' In 1871 the fees were fixed at the following levels:-

1/6 (7$^{1}/_{2}$p)	per quarter year for pupils in the beginners' class
2/- (10p)	per quarter year for pupils learning writing and elementary arithmetic
2/6 (12$^{1}/_{2}$p)	if also being taught elementary grammar, elementary geography and advanced arithmetic
3/- (15p)	if geography and grammar were at advanced level with bookkeeping also being taught

Fees for more advanced teaching were to be agreed between the teacher and the parents.

Linklater resigned in 1862 after a dispute over money which he alleged was owed to him by the Deacons' Court of the Church. He was succeeded by James C. Bruce from Glasgow who was given £1 to cover his travelling expenses to Rousay. He remained in the post for nine years, leaving when parents began to complain to the church authorities about the way he was running the school. It appears that his increasing unpopularity in Wasbister was reflected in the ever decreasing annual sums being collected for the support of the school. The vacancy caused by his departure was filled for four months by a local divinity student, William M. Craigie of Cogar, until the appointment of William McKay who had recently completed his training at Moray House Teachers' Training College in Edinburgh. The Deacons' Court agreed to the following stipulations made by McKay:-

1. that the advertised salary of £23 should be confirmed
2. that the Deacons' Court would fulfil all the conditions and supply all the apparatus necessary to ensure that the school be made up to, and maintained at, Government standards
3. that the scholars in attendance should pay a fee of not less than 1/6 (7$^{1}/_{2}$p) per quarter, to be paid weekly, monthly or quarterly

An agreement was reached with McKay that he would be responsible for cutting and preparing his peats himself and that the Wasbister farmers would cart them home for him. Some months earlier an application had been made to have the school put under government inspection and this had been agreed to provided water closets were installed. In the conditions that McKay laid down for accepting the post he was trying to ensure that the Free Kirk carried out the necessary improvements. The work was speedily carried out and it is recorded that the funds to pay for it were collected 'fairly easily' because the people of the district were pleased over the improvements at the school and the appointment of the new teacher. The sale of the crop grown on the school land in 1871 fetched the sum of £4.25 which was used to pay for a wooden floor in the schoolroom. On his first visit to the school H.M. Inspector recommended that an alteration be made to the teacher's desk which had formerly been used as a pulpit.

Two years later, in 1873, the Free Kirk School in Wasbister was taken over by the Rousay School Board.

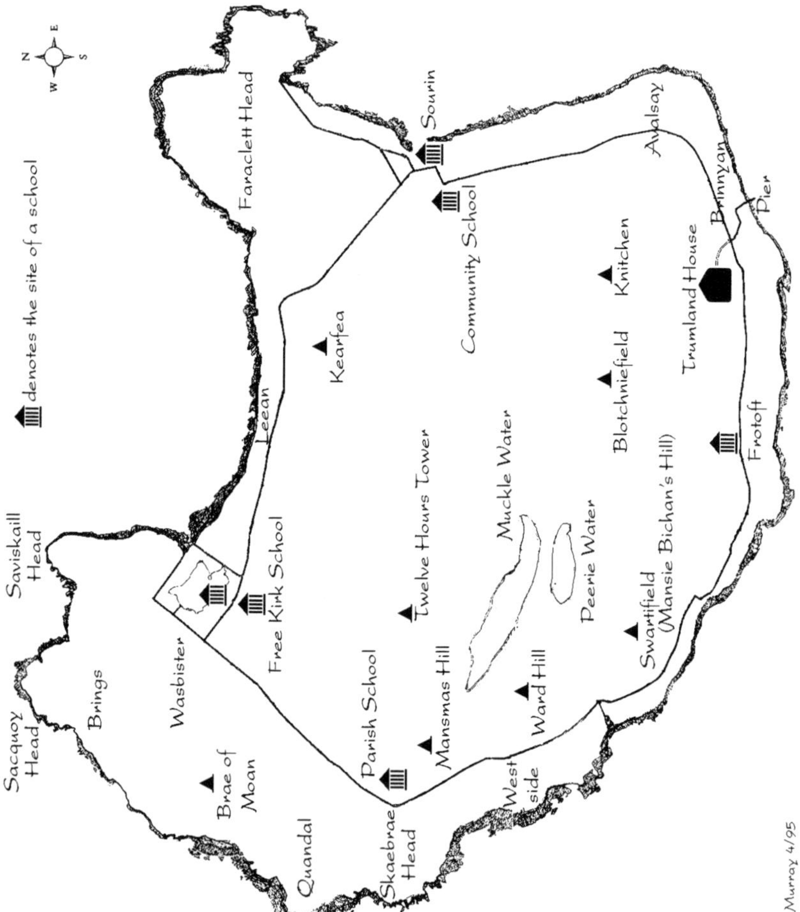

Sketch Map of Rousay

Rousay School Board

The Education (Scotland) Act of 1872 brought about important changes in Scottish education. It decreed that responsibility for providing and administering schools would lie with publicly elected School Boards. Another of its main provisions was that attendance at school would be compulsory for all children between the ages of 5 and 13 years. It was foreseen that a huge school building programme would be required throughout Scotland and government funding was set aside for this.

The School Boards took over in 1873. In Rousay an election was unnecessary as the number of nominations matched the five places on the Board. The members were General Burroughs, who owned almost all the island, James Sinclair of Newhouse, and the three local ministers, Rev. James Gardner of the Established Church, Rev. J. McLellan of the United Presbyterian Church, and Rev. Neil P. Rose of the Free Church. At the Board's first meeting Burroughs was appointed chairman, a post he would have regarded as his of right, given his position in the community.

One of the Board's first decisions was to conduct a census to ascertain how many children of school age there were in each district, and how many of them had been attending school. The information collected is shown in the Table 3.

Right at the outset the Board had a serious problem to deal with at each of the three schools on the island. At Sourin, a petition signed by the heads of 42 families and 10 others was submitted at the Board's first meeting. This asked for new school buildings and a 'thoroughly qualified teacher.' The widespread dissatisfaction with Mr. Reid was reflected in the poor attendance with only one child in four attending

Table 3 — Number of Children
Aged Between 5 and 13 Years

	Egilsay	**Frotoft**	**Sourin**	**Wasbister**	**Wyre**
No. in Census	39	45	83	55	16
No. at School	30	30	21	55	20

school. The inadequacy of the building, which had been provided by the SSPCK in 1725, must also have been a major factor in the low attendance rate. Ninety-five people in Wasbister signed a petition requesting a new school in that district. Three parents from Frotoft appeared at the Board's second meeting to demand the removal of their teacher, Sinclair McKay. They reported that in the district 'great dissatisfaction is prevalent against him.' This demand was backed up by a petition signed by 25 parents and 2 others.

The Board's response to the Sourin petition was 'to agree unanimously to declare the present buildings altogether inadequate, insufficient, and unsatisfactory, and the present teaching inefficient and unsatisfactory.' Within a few months permission was obtained from the Education Department in Edinburgh to build a new school on the opposite side of the road from the old one. General Burroughs was thanked by the Board for his generosity in charging only 1/-(5p) per year in feu duty on the new site. A proposal to pension off Reid, who had 30 years' service, with £10 a year was turned down by Edinburgh as he was only 52 years old. Eventually he left with a small pension paid by the church authorities in Edinburgh. The use of the Free Kirk was obtained to house the Sourin school until the new building was erected. A photograph of the time, taken outside the kirk, shows nearly 80 pupils in attendance. The foundation stone of the new school was laid by Burroughs in June, 1875 on the east side of the front door of the schoolhouse. Under it was placed a bottle containing a short history of the School Board, a document showing the estimated cost of the building, a copy of the new School Code, copies of local newspapers, and a few coins of the realm.

The Board accepted the views of the Wasbister parents that their building was inadequate and plans were made for the schoolroom to be enlarged and the lavatories improved but it appears that these plans were never put into effect because a decision was made in 1875 that a new school was going to be necessary. The new teacher, William Mckay, was achieving excellent results. The inspector, in his 1872 report on the school, recorded his 'confidence that the highly intelligent and painstaking teacher will remedy any faults before the next inspection.' The teacher recorded at the same time that he was finding the work very agreeable and was having no difficulty in maintaining discipline as the pupils were 'remarkably docile and affectionate.' He added that he always tried to enlist the sympathy of the older boys. He recorded that a pleasant atmosphere was created through his Christmas gift of fruit to the children, but his first Christmas on Rousay was described as being 'Dull! dull!'

At Frotoft, Sinclair McKay was finding it impossible to stand up to those who wanted rid of him. The School Board summoned him to a meeting to answer charges of inefficiency and negligence in his duties, and of being slovenly in appearance and habits. He was also accused of setting a bad example by smoking in school in the the presence of pupils. Having reached the age of 60, he wisely decided to retire and appears to have done so with a small pension. His successor was Angus McGillivray who was promised an annual salary of £75 plus a house and $1^1/_2$ acres of ground. Log books came into use in the Rousay schools in 1874, and an early entry in the Frotoft one recorded a visit paid to the school by the Rev. Neil Rose, the Clerk to the School Board. 'He remained a long time with us, much to the satisfaction of the scholars who really went with double energy to their work.' Mr. McGillivray clearly knew on which side his bread was buttered but it availed him little. Less than three years later he resigned after repeated requests to have his salary made up to £100 were turned down. He considered that he was entitled to the same level of salary as his Wasbister and Sourin colleagues who were being paid £100 but the Board apparently thought otherwise.

Shortly after taking over, the School Board realised that the Frotoft building was too small for the number of pupils in the district, which at that time was 45. Within a few years, another room was added at the rear of the building with a doorway being knocked through the back wall to give access to it. Other improvements made at that time included the fitting of a wooden ceiling in the main classroom and the provision of lavatories. It was at that time also that the Board decided to build dykes around the school playgrounds.

Despite the urgent need for a new school in Sourin, two years elapsed before building began. Meanwhile, Mr. James Inkster, who succeeded Mr. Reid at he beginning of 1874, had to manage as best he could in trying to run a school of 80 pupils in the uncomfortable and unsuitable conditions of the Free Kirk. Seven months after the foundation stone was laid, and at a cost of £669, the new school was ready for occupation and was officially opened by Burroughs on the twelfth of January, 1876. A soiree was held in the evening to celebrate the occasion. The two classrooms, one much smaller than the other, must have been packed to capacity to hold the 80 pupils on the roll at that time. However, a decline soon set in and the school never again had to accommodate that number of pupils.

Quarterly fees, set by the Board, were on a scale starting at $7^1/_2$p for Infants and rising to 20p for Standard VI pupils. Some relief from payment was given to large families. Where five or more children from the same family were of school age, fees were charged for only the four eldest. The abolition of fees in 1889 must have come as a great relief to many households and also to the teachers who were charged with the task of collecting them from families many of whom were not able to pay them.

Written work, especially among the younger classes, was done on slates but where jotters and exercise books were required the pupils had to provide their own. Another requirement placed upon the children of that time was for each of them to bring a peat to school each day for the classroom fire. Sometimes parents would withhold peats if they wished to express displeasure at something the teacher had done, not seeming to realise that he would not be the only one to suffer the subsequent cold. There were frequent complaints by the teachers about the inadequate provision for the cleaning of schools. The floor was swept only once a week and the windows cleaned only when the inspector's annual visit was imminent. At the new Sourin school the cleaning was done by one of the boys who, by way of reward, was excused from paying fees.

School hours fixed by the Board were from ten o'clock to four with an hour's break in the middle. This break could be shortened during the winter months. The first hour of each day had to be devoted to religious education with the Board specifying the biblical passages to be studied in each school during the year. Members of the Board visited each school annually to examine the pupils on this part of their studies. During the early years of compulsory schooling some parents continued to take a relaxed view of their children's absences from school. Boys were permitted to attend on only a half-time basis during the summer months if they were required at home for herding and other tasks, provided that they returned to full-time attendance at he time of the inspector's annual visit. Attendances fell away rapidly once the inspection was past. Teachers complained that pupils were seen no more as their thirteenth birthday drew near, and younger children failed to appear when they reached school age. So serious did the problem become that the Sourin teacher tendered his resignation, which he withdrew only when promised that the Board would do something about the poor attendances. What the Board did was to appoint a School Attendance Officer, then known as a Defaulting Officer or Compulsory Officer, in the person of John Gow who was Burroughs' gamekeeper. His appointment seemed to make little difference as complaints from the teachers about poor attendance continued for several years. Attendance was always adversely affected by bad weather. Few children would have had adequate waterproof clothing so parents wisely kept them at home on wet days instead of having them sitting in school in damp clothes.

The children eagerly looked forward to the annual picnic at Trumland House. A report in *The Orcadian* of August 1876 reported that 75 pupils from Sourin, 54 from Frotoft, 39 from Wasbister, and 18 from Wyre gathered at Trumland on a day of torrential rain. The Sourin contingent carried bannerettes, putting the others in the shade! On these happy occasions the General and Mrs. Burroughs, along with any house guests of the time, led the children through a programme of games and races followed by tea on the lawns. At the end of an enjoyable afternoon the children were sent home with a paper poke of goodies and a small gift which sometimes consisted of nothing more than a picture cut from a magazine.

Early in 1879 there was an outbreak of diphtheria in Rousay which was to last for most of the year. Eight or nine people died of the disease, most of them being children. Three of the children were from one family, the Leonards of Digro. Although the outbreak first appeared in Sourin, and most of the victims belonged to that district, the school there does not appear to have been closed till August, by which time there had been several deaths. The school then remained closed for the rest of the year. Most pupils were kept at home for much of that year as parents were convinced that children ran a greater risk of catching the dreaded disease if they attended school. There were deaths in Wasbister and Frotoft too, and although the Wasbister school was closed for a time early in the year, the Frotoft one remained open. Scarlet fever was also present in the island that year. The Frotoft teacher recorded that he took precautions against its spread by placing disinfectants in the school.

Rousay people were well served by the three teachers in post during the early 1870s. James Inkster in Sourin, William McKay in Wasbister, and Angus McGillvary in Frotoft were given excellent reports by H.M. Inspectors on their annual visits. Inkster's teaching was particularly highly thought of, drawing such comments as, 'The whole style and character of the work is first class,' and, 'Very satisfactory with some of the work being almost faultless.' All three were lost to the island when the Board refused to raise their salaries to the level the teachers demanded. The Board had to weigh these demands against the resources at its disposal. In the four years of its existence it had built new schools in Sourin, Egilsay, and Wyre as well as carrying out improvements at its other schools. Government grants covered most of the cost of new buildings and major improvements with the rest coming from the local education rate. Other income available to the Board stemmed from school fees and the government grants, the size of which depended on the results of the annual inspections. The grant for a school usually covered more than half the teacher's salary.

The badly needed new school at Wasbister was built on a site given by Burroughs from the farm of Cogar. The building was designed and erected by Alexander Gibson of Vacquoy at a cost of £495 and was officially opened by Burroughs on the first of November, 1881. The Board was well pleased with the new school, claiming that there was 'nothing to match it in Orkney or any rural area.' To mark the occasion, Mrs. Burroughs made a gift of fruit and a bun to each child.

During the early years of its existence the Rousay School Board managed its affairs with considerable skill and without disharmony amongst its members. The islanders recognised this, and when its term of office ended after three years, the Board was given another term without a poll being necessary. The same happened in 1879 and 1882 with the membership continuing to consist of Burroughs, the three ministers, and James Sinclair of Newhouse. Rev. Archibald McCallum had replaced Mr. Rose at the Free Kirk in 1880 and became a Board member. Latterly, some disharmony had crept in with the Free Kirk minister finding himself in a minority of one to four. This productive and relatively peaceful period in the Board's life came to an end with the approach of 1885 when its fourth term of office would be over.

Burroughs, with his regime of ever increasing rents, was not a popular landlord. The depth of his unpopularity was brought home to him at a meeting of the Napier Commission at Kirkwall in 1883. Lord Napier headed a Royal Commission set up to enquire into the conditions of crofters in the Highlands and Islands. The Rousay crofters, ably led by James Leonard of Digro, and assisted by McCallum, told the Commission of the harsh regime Burroughs imposed upon his tenants. Unlike other lairds, Burroughs refused to give an undertaking not to take action against those who spoke out against him to the Commission. Burroughs would not forgive those who had spoken out, and within weeks he had taken action against two crofters who had done so. James Leonard, who had taken the lead in organising and presenting the crofters' case, and James Grieve, who had supported him, were evicted from their crofts at Digro and Outerdykes.

Feelings ran high after Napier's visit and the subsequent evictions, and the islanders split into two camps. On the one hand were the crofters who had the strong backing of the Free Kirk and its minister, and on the other, all those who supported Burroughs. They included his employees and most of the large farmers. Unfortunately, the School Board was to be the arena in which the two sides were to conduct their battles which, for the most part, had nothing to do with education.

At the 1885 election for the School Board Leonard topped the poll, with McCallum coming second, and Burroughs third. The other two successful candidates were James Johnston who represented the Egilsay estate interests and John Craigie of Hullion who was the island postmaster. Both of them were looked upon as supporters of Burroughs but Craigie frequently followed an independent line at Board meetings. The Board moved quickly against George McCrie whom it employed as clerk and treasurer. A native of Edinburgh, McCrie, then in his mid-30s, had lived in Rousay on an annuity for several years, boarding at Curquoy. In addition to his School Board job, he also held the post of Inspector of the Poor, in which capacity he was seen as a laird's man. Burroughs threatened to resign if the Board dismissed McCrie. It was a threat he had to carry out at the next meeting when Craigie voted with Leonard and McCallum for the dismissal. McCallum became chairman and the Board decided to fill the vacancy by co-option. A move to appoint the unsuccessful candidate with the highest number of votes at the recent election was rejected, and James Grieve, the other evicted crofter, became the new member. The crofters' position on the Board was further strengthened shortly afterwards when Johnston and Craigie resigned, the latter over the Board's determination to be rid of the Sourin and Wasbister teachers who had fallen into disfavour with the crofters. Johnston was replaced by Hugh Marwick of Guidal, a move that gave the crofters control of the Board.

In the troubles that flared up in Rousay in the aftermath of Napier's visit, a letter which threatened his life was received by Burroughs who reported the matter to the authorities at Kirkwall. Two Sourin boys were suspected of writing it, and the Procurator Fiscal, armed with a warrant, arrived at the Sourin school and demanded of the teacher, Mr. Moyes, to be allowed to examine the children's copy books in an attempt to identify the culprits. In the face of such authority Moyes had little choice and presented the books for inspection. From that day on, Moyes was a marked man in the eyes of the crofters several of whom had had earlier disagreements with him over school fees and the punishment of their children. The Wasbister teacher, William Cooper, had received quite a good report from the inspector in 1885 after three years of unfavourable ones but it was not enough to save him. The Board's reasons for wishing to be rid of him probably had less to do with his teaching abilities than with the fact that he was married to the daughter of John Gibson of Langskaill who was one of Burroughs' leading supporters in the island. For procedural reasons, the Board did not manage to dismiss Moyes and Cooper until the late summer of 1886. McCallum, who was both clerk and chairman at that time, visited both schools and made entries in the logbooks to the effect that the teachers were no longer in charge. One wonders whether this was the only method adopted of informing the teachers of their dismissal.

After the 1888 election, the crofters still held the majority of places on the School Board and again voted McCallum into the chair. Within a year, however, he had left the island and Rev. Alexander Pirie of the U.P. Kirk became chairman of the Board. The people of Rousay, and particularly their schools, had been poorly served by the School Board during the four years of McCallum's chairmanship. The rapid turnover of teachers who found it impossible to work effectively under a dictatorial and inefficient Board made for unsettled conditions in the schools and adversely affected the children's schooling. For the crofters, it has to be said that their activities on the School Board were not primarily concerned with education but with conducting a battle against an oppressive laird and his supporters. The School Board was the only arena in which crofters and laird met on equal terms, and once they had won control of it, the crofters, under McCallum's destructive influence, gave no quarter to their opponents. After McCallum's departure the Board adopted more moderate policies under Pirie's chairmanship and gradually the Board's relationship with its teachers began to improve.

The school leaving age went up to 14 years in 1883 but until 1901 pupils could be allowed to leave at 13 if an examination showed that they had reached the fifth standard. Pupils of 10 years and over who had reached the third standard were allowed to be away from school from May to October if they were needed at home for herding, working the peats, or helping with the harvest. One strictly observed condition was that such pupils had to return to school at the time of the inspector's visit in June or July because the amount of the annual government grant depended on their being present for assessment. Teachers frequently complained that other pupils, besides the herds, absented themselves after the inspector's visit. The main school holidays, lasting seven weeks, were taken in September and October. One or two days were taken at Christmas and a few more around New Year's Day. This pattern remained unchanged till 1922 when the main holiday was moved to cover July and early August. Two weeks were given at harvest time and a week at the New Year. It was not until 1933 that the present practice of including both Christmas Day and New Year's Day in the winter break was introduced.

The poor attendance record of Sourin pupils continued to cause annoyance and frustration to a succession of teachers there. The problem was of long standing, dating back to pre-School Board days when attendance was voluntary. An outbreak of any infectious disease such as diphtheria, scarlet fever, whooping cough or influenza practically emptied a school because children were kept at home, out of the way of possible infection. Quite often the school remained closed for the duration of the outbreak. An entry in the Sourin logbook in 1890 records that the school books of a family returning to school after a bout of scarlet fever were destroyed and new ones issued. It was not uncommon for not a single pupil to turn up on very wet days. On top of these excusable absences successive teachers in Sourin had to contend with absences that were unacceptable. The problem was frequently brought to the notice of the Board which always appeared reluctant to risk possible unpopularity by taking effective action to remedy matters. Certain unpopularity befell any teacher who was thought to be making too frequent use of the services of the Compulsory Officer to chase up defaulters. In 1900 the Sourin teacher recorded an unusually high attendance of 94%, followed by the comment, 'I punished those who were absent through their parents' carelessness. Hence the good attendance.' A year later he reported that the senior pupils appeared to be allowed by their parents to attend or not as they wished. In 1903 not one of the older pupils was attending school. By 1909 the position was rather better with all the pupils being present on two days in the same week, the first time that had happened in a year. A logbook entry in 1925 shows that the attendance rarely reached 90% for a week.

A dramatic improvement in the Sourin attendance took place in 1927 with the arrival of Miss Isabel G. Craigie, M.A. to take charge of the senior classes:

August, 1928	Attendances now regularly over 90%
December, 1928	School concert held in hall. Great success. Attendance for that week 100% — a record.
September, 1929	Attendance for week 99.5% although harvest in full swing.
October, 1929	Attendance keeping up. Harvesting not affecting it.

It had taken nearly sixty years for the people of Sourin to accept compulsory school attendance!

The Sourin teachers were not the only ones who found it difficult to put up with poor attendances. Their Frotoft and Wasbister colleagues continually complained when large numbers of their pupils disappeared from school for five months of the year to do herding and other tasks on the farms. They also complained about the absences at times of inclement weather and when an infectious disease appeared in the district, but they probaly found them more acceptable than the herds' absences. Like Sourin, Frotoft and Wasbister were slow to accept compulsory schooling. In 1876, three years after compulsory schooling came in, the average attendance at Wasbister was only 49.5%. However, that state of affairs did not last, and the people of Frotoft and Wasbister saw the error of their ways much sooner than did their Sourin neighbours.

From its inception the School Board had been urged by the Department of Education in Edinburgh to employ women teachers in all its schools except Sourin. The reason for this was that women were paid at a much lower rate than their male colleagues. In 1879 the men teachers at Sourin and Wasbister were being paid £100 per year. Forty years later the salaries of the women teachers in the three schools had still not risen beyond £85. Nevertheless, more than twenty years were to pass before the Board heeded Edinburgh's advice and the first female teacher appeared in Rousay. She was Mrs. Simpson, wife of the Sourin Teacher, who was appointed to Frotoft in 1894. Except for a few short, temporary appointments, Frotoft was not to have any more male teachers. The first appointment of a woman teacher at Wasbister followed five years later, and all her successors were also women. Jessie Marwick from Guidal was the first woman to take charge at Sourin. She took over in 1903, and it was not until 1934 that another male appointment was made. Jessie had been a pupil at Sourin and was appointed Pupil Teacher there in 1887, completing her training four years later. During her early training she was frequently late in the morning and the teacher recorded that he had had to speak to her about the matter on several occasions. In her final year of training, and before reaching her eighteenth birthday, she was given charge of the school for two months between the departure of one teacher and the arrival of the next. Her brother, Hugh, succeeded her as Pupil Teacher, the first step in his distinguished career as scholar and writer.

An assistant teacher was first employed at Sourin in 1905, and it remained a two-teacher school almost continuously until the outbreak of the Second World War. It was not to have two teachers again until the new school opened in 1960.

At each school the Board employed someone to teach knitting and sewing to the girls, and from time to time Wasbister was allowed a Pupil

Teacher. One who held that post was James G. Craigie who was appointed in 1876 at the age of fourteen. About ten years later he took over the paid position of clerk to the Board, and remained in that post until School Boards were abolished in 1918. For over thirty years, whenever a temporary teaching vacancy occurred in Rousay, Egilsay or Wyre, arising either from illness or a change of teacher, 'The Clerk,' as he was generally known, stepped in to keep the school going. After the new Wasbister school was opened the Craigies moved into the old schoolhouse which was renamed Ivybank and James set up a merchant's business in the old schoolroom. A fire destroyed the shop in the early 1920s. It was later re-roofed and used as a joiner's shop. 'The Clerk' died in 1927.

School Boards were abolished in 1918 and the control of all the schools in the county passed to the Education Committee of Orkney County Council.

School Stamps

Rousay Schools 1918-1960

By the time the School Board came to the end of its days, the children at the three schools were following a full curriculum consisting not only of the three basics, reading, writing and arithmetic, but also English grammar and composition, spelling and dictation, history, geography. music, drawing and painting, and R.E. While girls learned sewing and knitting, boys were engaged in some kind of handicraft such as raffia work. In addition to all that, the teachers, some of them just newly out of college, would find time to prepare their pupils for a concert given to an appreciative audience of parents. It was common for a concert to be combined with a Christmas party, and followed by a dance. Such an event was one of the two highlights of the children's year. The other was the picnic, an afternoon of fun and races for the children followed by a number of novelty races for the grown-ups. Given threepence for being first in a race, tuppence for second, and a penny for third, wealthy indeed was the child who went home that night clutching twelve or more precious pennies in a sweaty hand. In mid-afternoon the children were given milk and a paper bag of goodies to keep them going till the hand around tea appeared after the sports were over. Some of the adults then went home to attend to the evening milking. By the time they returned, young men and women from other districts were arriving and the dancing was getting under way. A charge made for the dance defrayed expenses and left something over to pay for the party the following Christmas.

The days of pupils being allowed to stay off school to do herding were long since past. Attendances were good and some children began to take pride in being among the most regular attenders. In the 1930s, Clara Donaldson, a pupil at Wasbister, left school at the age of fourteen with a record of perfect attendance. Up until a few years earlier any pupil achieving this record had received a watch from the Education Committee, but this practice had been discontinued by the time Clara reached leaving age. She did, however, receive a watch, bought for her by her teacher, Miss Mathieson, at her own expense.

The pattern of school holidays changed in 1957 when the long-established practice of closing rural schools for three weeks in autumn came to an end. With more and more machines coming on to the farms the need for children's help in the harvest field was decreasing. Parents who considered that their children's assistance at harvest time was still essential had to apply to the Education Committee for the necessary exemption from school.

A few years after schools came under the control of the County Education Committee, post-Primary pupils were grouped in Advanced Divisions. Pupils passed into the Advanced Division through the Qualifying examination which they sat as they approached the age of twelve. At that stage a few opted to continue their education at Kirkwall Grammar School but the number of Rousay pupils at Kirkwall at any one time between the two world wars could be counted on the fingers of one hand. Most moved into the Advanced Division at their local school, but some transferred to Sourin where a wider choice of subjects was on offer. The Inspector's report for 1932 commended the introduction of Science and Latin teaching at Sourin and hoped that cooking would soon follow. Cooking did soon follow, but only for boys while the girls were at needlework. Some former pupils, now in their seventies, can date their first attempts at making an omelette, or chips, or pancakes to Mr. Wallace's cookery lessons in the 1930s. He also taught the older boys some simple metalwork. This consisted of making some useful household articles out of tin and included learning how to solder. Woodwork classes for older boys began in Sourin in 1957 with William M. Craigie, a local joiner, as instructor. Boys from Wasbister and Frotoft were transported to Sourin by car twice a week to take part in these lessons. The teacher recorded that the class had been going for a month before a supply of wood arrived, and it then lay at the pier for a while awaiting transport.

The buildings were well maintained with repairs and minor improvements carried out on a regular basis. The classrooms were redecorated every few years with the woodwork being revarnished and the walls and ceilings given another coat of distemper. The walls were wood lined to a height of four feet, level with the window sills. Several oil lamps were suspended from the ceiling on long wires but they were seldom lit. If it became too dark, near the end of the day, for schoolwork to continue the children were sent home early. The teacher's desk stood on a small raised platform about nine inches high. About 1930, long desks which held several pupils were replaced with two-seater ones that had hinged seats. When not needed for written work the desk top folded back to form a book rest. Beneath the top, and in front of the pupil's knees, there was a U-shaped rack for holding books and jotters. Slots to accommodate slates were cut in the front edge of the desk top and there were also two holes for inkwells.

Emphasis was placed on the need to produce good handwriting and a weekly lesson was devoted to it. For the youngest pupils the lessons were more frequent. Copy books were in use at all stages. At the top of each page was a line of beautiful copperplate writing which the pupil was asked to reproduce as accurately as possible on the rest of the page. Early attempts at using pen and ink usually ended in inky fingers and unsightly ink blots marring the pupil's best effort in the copy book. At the annual flower show, prizes were awarded for the best examples of handwriting from the three schools, and much earnest effort was put in by the older pupils in trying to produce an immaculate copy of the first verse of the national anthem.

Each of the Rousay schools had a glass-fronted bookcase holding the Coats Library. Similar libraries and bookcases were gifted to 4,000 schools by the philanthropist James Coats of the Paisley thread-making firm J. & P. Coats. The Wasbister school had a smaller bookcase of encyclopedias which also had come from Mr. Coats.

At the start of the war in 1939, the assistant teacher was withdrawn from Sourin because the roll was falling and the teacher was needed elsewhere to replace one of those called up for military service. Women teachers, who had been required to resign from their posts on getting married, were called back to service. Among them was Mrs. Lydia Corsie, formerly Miss Baikie, who was brought in to fill temporary vacancies at Sourin. Another was Mrs. Isabel Grieve, formerly Miss Craigie, who did temporary duty at Wasbister and later taught at Frotoft for eleven years.

Table 4 shows the extent of the fall in the school population in Rousay which started not long after school attendance became compulsory in 1873. By the turn of the century the number of pupils had halved, and by 1940 had more than halved again leaving a total of only 40 spread over the three schools. In the 1950s plans were laid for the closure of the schools in Frotoft and Wasbister and for the transfer of their pupils to a new school to be built in Sourin.

Work began in October, 1958. A wooden hut was erected in the Sourin playground to accommodate the pupils during the erection of the new school. The building which had been opened by Burroughs 82 years earlier was demolished, leaving the schoolhouse standing on

Table 4 — School Rolls

Frotoft		Sourin		Wasbister	
Year	Roll	Year	Roll	Year	Roll
1873	47	1873	83	1873	71
1883	37	1874	78	1874	65
1890	53	1878	71	1884	51
1891	39	1885	55	1887	46
1900	23	1886	62	1892	43
1925	17	1893	46	1901	28
1933	7	1908	40	1907	22
1937	5	1927	44	1914	22
1942	9	1933	44	1925	26
1944	10	1939	26	1931	19
1945	12	1940	19	1933	16
1951	15	1945	13	1941	11
		1948	18	Records missing after 1943.	
		1952	15		
		1954	21		
		1956	23		
		1956	17		

its own for a short time. Who was the boy (or girl) who, at some time during those 82 years, spied a narrow gap between the floorboards, and, when the opportunity arose, posted the teacher's strap through it? It remained in its hiding place until the demolition men uncovered it.

From all three schools come stories of the teacher's strap going missing. The Wasbister one went astray after a concert and was found by the roadmen a few months later when they were cleaning out a ditch

200 yards from the school. On another occasion someone threw it up through the hatch into the loft and it was not found until much later. Some of the bigger boys at Wasbister must have been proud of their ability to take punishment without flinching for they got hold of the strap at lunchtime one day and started laying into each other with it to see who could take the most 'palms.' One boy took eighteen before giving in. When the teacher came in she somehow found out that something improper had been going on but not exactly what. She gave each of the boys involved one stroke each, but by that time it had little effect on their stinging fingers. It was not only for bad behaviour that the strap was used. Some teachers used it for failure to learn regardless of whether that failure was due to lack of effort or lack of ability. It is little wonder that the pupils sometimes dared to remove from the scene what one teacher referred to as the leather medicine.

The three 19th century buildings served their communities well, not only as schools, but also as centres for community activities such as concerts, dances, whist drives, sales of work, and meetings of local organisations. They acted as community centres long before that term came into common usage. The pre-School Board Frotoft building, with its lower walls and more lowly pitched roof, was the smallest and least imposing of the three schools. It was sold along with the schoolhouse and has been converted to provide extra rooms for what is now a very attractive house. Early in the century, the exterior of the Sourin building was cement plastered, presumably to deal with a dampness problem. This concealed the variety of colouring and shading in the stonework and detracted from the appearance of the building. Of the three buildings the most pleasing to the eye was the Wasbister one. An attractive decorative feature that it had was a finial placed at the midpoint of the roof ridge. This cast iron structure, seen in photograph 9, was removed after being damaged in a storm in the 1940s. The building, which is still in the ownership of the County, now houses the island's snooker club.

PRESENTED

TO

Wasbister Public School

BY

JAMES COATS, JR., ESQ.,

FERGUSLIE HOUSE, PAISLEY.

1906.

No................

☞ ***Books must be kept clean.***

Coats Book Label

Rousay Community School

The new school at Sourin was opened on the 26th of August, 1960. Only 20 months in the building, Rousay Junior Secondary School was a palace compared with its predecessor. The large hall was fitted with a stage which doubled as a cloakroom. There were three classrooms, one of which had a science lab annexe. Another was used for woodwork and the Infants occupied the third. A kitchen and a staffroom which doubled as an office were also provided. The greatest advance of all, in the sight of many pupils, must have been the provision of inside toilets. Long past were the days when H.M. Inspector had complained of the 'gross accumulations in the offices.' Gone too were the days of oil lamps and smokey stoves that failed to heat the old schoolrooms even on moderately cold days. Mains power was still a few years away from Rousay but the new school had its own electricity generator. The school log records that the central heating system that was installed proved not to be the boon that had been hoped for, because it was continually breaking down. This continued for many years until a new system was eventually installed.

Its roll of Primary and Secondary pupils, drawn from the whole island, numbered 35. Mr. G.A. Nelson was the headmaster, and Mrs. Lily Miller the assistant teacher. In addition, Mr. W. Craigie was engaged to teach woodwork and metalwork for 4 hours per week, Mrs. J.S. Gibson to teach needlework for 2 hours, and Mrs. Firth to teach music for 1 hour. A janitor and two kitchen workers were also appointed. It was recorded that 100 meals were consumed during the first week. At a later stage, the cook, Miss M. Taylor gave cookery lessons to the secondary girls, and the metalwork classes were taken over by Mr. John Craigie who was also the janitor.

Within a month of the school opening, the secondary pupils along with those from Primary 7 were off on an educational visit to Birsay, Skara Brae, and Maeshowe in connection with their study of Early Civilisations. This was the first recorded visit by Rousay pupils to places of interest outside the island. Such visits are now common, with pupils sometimes travelling far afield outside Orkney.

With Mr. James Merriman's appointment as head teacher in 1962 there began a period of joint activities with the Egilsay and Wyre schools. Joint sports days were held and all three schools pooled their talents for Christmas concerts. Fund raising events also got under way. The first sale of work organised by the school raised £80 towards the purchase price of a television set.

When the new school opened in 1960 there were 9 pupils in the secondary department. The number quickly fell and at the end of 1963, when only one secondary pupil remained at school, the classes in woodwork and metalwork were discontinued. By the start of the 1966-67 session the number had climbed to six, including two from Wyre, but no secondary pupils remained after Christmas, 1968. It was at that time that the decision was taken to close the secondary department for good.

Rousay children who wished to follow more academic courses than those on offer in the island had traditionally transferred to Kirkwall Grammar School, usually at the end of their Primary schooling. Some may have stayed with relatives in town, but for most children, it involved going into lodgings. This must have been a traumatic experience for many isles' children who were unaccustomed to being away from their own small communities, The agonies of home-sickness passed eventually and they could look forward to getting home at the end of term.

In the 1950s the Education Committee took over part of the former Post Office hostel in Old Scapa Road as a school hostel for girls. Boys still had to go into digs. A purpose-built hostel was opened in the early 1970s to accommodate all the isles' pupils attending school in Kirkwall.

By the late 1950s, changes in transport arrangements made it possible for the Rousay pupils at Kirkwall to get home at weekends unless weather conditions made it impossible for the boat to cross. When it became necessary for all secondary pupils to go to Kirkwall, parental pressure forced the Education Committee to bear the transport costs of weekend visits home to Rousay. Improved ferry provision in the 1990s make it possible for Rousay children to commute daily to school in Kirkwall, with transport costs being borne by the Committee. A few prefer to stay in the hostel, travelling home only at weekends, but most of the younger pupils travel daily.

Photograph 1 — Sourin Public School (1876-1958).

Photograph 2 — Frotoft Public School.

Photograph 3 — Interior of Sourin Public School (1951).

Photograph 4 — Wasbister Public School.

Photograph 5 — Rousay Community School.

Photograph 6 — James G. Craigie, 'The Clerk' (on the left).

Photograph 7 — Hugh Marwick. From a portrait by Stanley Cursiter. Reproduced by permission of Orkney Islands Council.

Photograph 8 — Sourin School circa 1913.

Photograph 9 — A Picnic Day at the Wasbister School in the late 1920s.

Photograph 10 — Sourin School 1929/30.

Photograph 11 — Wasbister School 1931.

Photograph 12 — Frotoft School 1936.

Photograph 13 — Sourin School 1936.

Photograph 14 — Wasbister School 1939.

Photograph 15 — Wasbister School 1947.

Photograph 16 — Frotoft School 1951.

Photograph 17 — Sourin School 1952/3.

Photograph 18 — Wasbister School 1956.

Photograph 19 — Rousay Community School 1961.

Photograph 20 — Rousay Community School Primary 2/3 1994.

Photograph 21 — Rousay Community School Senior Class 1994.

After the ending of secondary education on the island, Rousay Primary School came into being. By that time the roll was down to 15, less than half of what it had been nine years earlier. As such a small roll did not justify having two teachers, Mr Newell was transferred to another school in 1969 and the assistant, Miss Williams (later Mrs. Grieve), took charge of the school. Three years later, an increased roll brought about a return of the school's 2-teacher status. The roll rose to 30 in 1974, 35 in 1977, and 42 in 1978. Wyre children started coming to Rousay when the small school there was closed down in 1977, but they had little effect on the Rousay numbers. The roll dropped again all through the 1980s and had fallen back to a low point of 15 by 1990 before starting to rise once more. At the time of writing (1994), a third teacher has been appointed to cope with the increased roll.

The public hall, erected by ex-servicemen after World War 1, served the island well for thirty years until it was demolished by a hurricane in the early 1950s. Its successor, provided by the County Council, was a prefabricated building which also served its purpose as a community centre for thirty years until it fell into a state of disrepair. It was seen that it would be foolish to spend large sums of money on refurbishing or replacing it when the nearby school already provided many of the facilities that were required for community use. A small extension and some interior alterations at the school would provide all the facilities needed in a community centre and would, at the same time, enhance the facilities available for school use. The work that was necessary to bring about these changes must have caused considerable disruption to the work of the school. No doubt, both teachers and pupils were glad when it was over and they could return to normal working.

Rousay Community School was officially opened in October, 1984 by George Stevenson, Vice-Convener of Orkney Islands Council. Dr. Pearson, Chairman of the Community Association, accepted the building on behalf of the people of Rousay. An entry in the school logbook a few weeks later records that 'the premises are in use on most evenings and the new facilities are much appreciated by members of the community.' The new facilities include two general purposes rooms which can be made into one by pushing back a folding partition. One of these rooms has a small kitchen annexe. The main hall has had its large, fixed stage removed and that space has been converted to a storage area housing the hall chairs, the pack-away stage, and other large pieces of equipment. The community rooms are available for school use at times when they are not needed by any of the island's organisations. With a willingness on all sides to give and take, this arrangement seems to work well, and it is reported that disputes between the school and community organisations, concerning the shared facilities, do not arise.

Occasions when old and young combine forces for their mutual enjoyment occur when the senior citizens of the island gather at the school for lunch once a month. The children take pleasure in serving the meal and in entertaining the old people afterwards with any songs or recitations they have been learning. These old people must marvel at the cheerful and comfortable surroundings in which they find themselves, compared with the drab and draughty schoolrooms of their childhood. When they are invited into a classroom to hear from the children about some project they have just completed, they must marvel too at the variety of the curricular diet on offer, and at the richness of the school environment in which the children live and work and learn.

Above the entrance to the school hall there is a Stanley Cursiter portrait of Dr. Hugh Marwick, painted in oils, which was presented to the school by his widow in 1975. Born half a mile away, at Guidal, in 1882, Hugh Marwick received his early education at Sourin Public School. He went on to become a distinguished scholar and writer, and held the post of Director of Education in Orkney for many years. In that capacity, he frequently visited his old school. His visits were probably more frequent than the pupils would have wished, for he was fond of using these occasions to put them through their paces in arithmetic, grammar, or some other subject. After such a session with Dr. Marwick, some were left with the impression that the depth of their ignorance was truly abysmal. However, all would agree that it is fitting that a portrait of Rousay's most distinguished son should hang in the school in his native island, where it forms a link with the old school he had attended, and with even older schools, particularly the one across the road, stretching back to 1725.

Gleanings from the School Logbooks

WASBISTER	15 Jan 1872	Commenced a Latin class of 8 pupils.
WASBISTER	1 Feb 1872	The scholars render cheerful obedience.
WASBISTER	27 Feb 1872	Holiday of thanksgiving on account of the convalesence of the Prince of Wales.
WASBISTER	14 May 1872	The scholars can now sing fairly so we can now lighten the work occasionally with a song.
WASBISTER	14 April 1873	Sewing continues to improve. Much needed here as no indoor industrial work is taught at home.
SOURIN	11 Dec 1874	Thanksgiving day for harvest. No teaching.
WASBISTER	18 Feb 1874	Holiday on account of first ploughing match in the island.
FROTOFT	3 July 1874	It is really amusing how the pupils are put about when a stranger enters the school.
SOURIN	23 April 1875	Teacher felt unwell all week. Two of the senior boys had to give out the lessons one day. Not much progress made.
SOURIN	12 July 1875	Four days' holiday given after the annual inspection.
WASBISTER	8 June 1876	Children seem to find school a pleasure.

FROTOFT	21 July 1876	Requested scholars to provide themselves with such text books as are used by us.
SOURIN	1 Sept 1876	Board members visited school to conduct Religious Knowledge exams. Dismissed school at 5 o'clock.
SOURIN	H.M.I. report for 1878	Offices (lavatories) in an utterly disgraceful state. Board must appoint someone to remove the gross accumulations.
WASBISTER	16 Aug 1878	Two pupils have died of throat disease.
FROTOFT	14 Feb1879	French and Latin classes begun.
SOURIN	18 July 1879	Diphtheria, that dreadful malady, has again broken out and one scholar has died.
WASBISTER	17 Aug 1881	Annual picnic at Trumland House. Left school at 12.25 and arrived Trumland at 3. Left for home at 6.
SOURIN	2 Dec 1881	The Board to give half-a-crown to the boy and girl making the most attendances.
WASBISTER	9 May 1884	Seven more pupils left for herding this week. As usual they are the most backward probably owing to former absences.
SOURIN	25 July 1884	Half day on Wednesday as teacher away round the island with his father.
SOURIN	19 Dec 1884	School closed for a day to allow teacher to attend a funeral. Opened on Saturday to make up the attendance.
SOURIN	14 Aug 1885	Mrs. Burroughs called to give each child a bun and a bag in lieu of the usual picnic at Trumland.
FROTOFT	2 July 1886	Mrs. Pirie and Miss Mackay visited school to show pupils the writing desk purchased by pupils as a testamonial for Mr. Purdie (a teacher who had left).
SOURIN	25 Nov 1887	Want of proper lesson books is a very great drawback.
FROTOFT	10 Feb 1890	General and Mrs. Burroughs visited the school and hung up some pictures for the children.

FROTOFT	8 Aug 1890	Pail provided for girls to wash their hands in before Sewing.
SOURIN	17 July 1891	Floor not swept for two weeks.
WASBISTER	19 Feb 1897	School closed for eight weeks because of whooping cough.
SOURIN	4 March 1898	I find a great difficulty in maintaining proper discipline. I can't work much longer under this opposition.
FROTOFT	25 June 1900	Teacher got telegram from H.M. Inspector in the morning saying he would arrive at 3 pm. Arrived just after 5 and stayed till 7.30.
WASBISTER	14 April 1905	School holiday for funeral of General Burroughs.
SOURIN	17 Nov 1911	A new subject has been started — Mathematics.
SOURIN	24 Nov 1911	Algebra seems to be understood but greatest difficulty is with the Euclid.
SOURIN	12 June 1912	Two enamel pails for drinking water have been supplied. Filled every second day by cleaner.
WASBISTER	3 July 1913	First mention of medical inspection of pupils.
WASBISTER	Aug 1914	Teacher takes on the cleaning of school for £4 per annum.
WASBISTER	Jan 1918	School closed for 3 weeks because of exceptionally severe and prolonged snowstorms.
FROTOFT	30 June 1924	Piano gifted to school by Mrs. Walter G. Grant.
WASBISTER	Sept 1927	£120 raised at a bazaar for which pupils had made articles. Proceeds used to buy pianos for Wasbister and Sourin.
FROTOFT	8 March 1929	Twenty minutes given to singing of hymn, repetition of catechism, and bible reading every morning by order of the Education Committee.
FROTOFT	6 Sept 1929	Water filter supplied so that tank water can be drunk by pupils.

SOURIN	26 Oct 1929	Ringworm breaks out from time to time and usually spreads to other children in the family.
SOURIN	7 Feb 1931	The outhouses (lavatories) were today lime-washed and the holes made by rats were filled up with cement.
SOURIN	3 Dec 1934	A subscription list has been opened in the school to enable children who wish to do so to contribute to the national wedding gift to the Duke of Kent.
SOURIN	15 Feb 1935	Pupils in the senior room listened to a schools broadcast for the first time. Other early broadcasts listened to:
	11/11/1935	Armistice service from the Cenotaph, London.
	22/1/1936	Proclamation of Accession of King Edward VIII.
	28/1/1936	Funeral of King George V. School was officially closed but some pupils and some adults came to listen to broadcast.
	24/3/1936	Departure of the Queen Mary from the Clyde after its completion at John Brown's shipyard.
SOURIN	26 June 1936	Pupils in Primary Room spent an hour in Nature Study down at the shore while older pupils climbed Keirfea. An enjoyable and instructive outing.
FROTOFT	16 April 1937	Toilet paper and holders received from Medical Officer. One fixed in the girls' lavatory and one in the boys' lavatory.
FROTOFT	10 Nov 1939	Correspondence course begun for Advanced Division pupils. (The course was run from Kirkwall as a wartime measure.)
FROTOFT	8 Nov 1940	School hours during winter — 9.45 am till 2.45 pm.
WASBISTER	June 1941	Mr. Pirie, Head Air Raid Precautions warden for Rousay, called at school to test the children's gas masks.

FROTOFT	14 June 1941	Pupils attended school today, Saturday, so that the attendances for the year would reach 400.
FROTOFT	20 Mar 1942	Gift of seeds for school garden received from British War Relief Society in U.S.A.
WASBISTER	June 1942	The soap ration allowed to this school per month is 1 lb. of soft, a qr. lb. of hard, and a qr. lb. of toilet.
SOURIN	23 Jan 1953	Ian Donaldson allowed off school to compete in tractor ploughing match.
SOURIN	14 June 1957	Great activity this week when the mobile dental unit visited the school.
FROTOFT	18 Nov 1957	One pupil conveyed by car to Sourin for afternoon of woodwork.
SOURIN	25 Sept 1959	A local affliction known unprofessionally as the 'Rousay Sickness' has affected the pupils this week.
SOURIN	Nov 1959	A janitor has been appointed for the new school, entry into whose portals should be around January 1960.
June 1965		Pupils are to receive supplies of bottled milk. Janitor will collect it from the pier.
Sept 1966		Several children are absent after attending a wedding reception.
Jan 1967		Now connected to hydro-electric power. Much quieter in school since generator went out of use.
June 1967		Whole school made educational visit to Eynhallow travelling from Hullion by Tom Sinclair's boat. The visit was combined with a picnic and sports, and all the children (and staff!) enjoyed paddling in the sea and making sand-castles while waiting for the boat to return at 4 o'clock.
April 1973		First of our weekly visits to the Kirkwall swimming pool. Egilsay and Wyre children with us.

Feb 1975	A school savings group (pupil operated) has been started.
May 1977	A colour TV has been installed. The school had to contribute £50 to the cost.
May 1978	The KGS Rector and Hostel Warden came to talk to the pupils who will transfer to Kirkwall in August.
Dec 1984	We took delivery of a BBC computer this week.
Dec 1986	Two Wyre pupils were unable to return home because of the weather conditions and stayed overnight in the schoolhouse.
Feb 1988	All the members of the school visited the ferry Eynhallow to take part in a life jacket practice. We were even given a practical demonstration of the life jacket in use in the water. Most worthwhile.
July 1988	Whole school went for a picnic lunch up at 'High Robbie.'

Tales out of School

I was at the Sourin school for about four years before moving to the Mainland. Otto Thomson was the teacher at that time. He was a keen radio ham and had his station set up in one of the upstairs rooms of the schoolhouse. I remember some of us being taken up there one day to see this amateur radio station. We spoke over the air to someone in Norway that day. Mr. Thomson also had some radio controlled boats that he sailed on the loch of Quoys. Another model that he had was a plane that flew around on a thin control wire. Some of the bigger boys built a model plane under his instruction but I don't know if it ever flew.

There's one incident from my schooldays that I remember fairly well. I had gone home with Hugh Mainland to his house after school. We were about 8 or 9 at the time. We walked over to Ham where we found an old boat lying up on the shore. We learned later it had been there for many years and was highly unseaworthy. We managed to get it afloat and clambered in, completely undaunted by the fact that there was only one oar. We drifted out from the shore and before long the tide caught us and was carrying us out towards the Holm of Scockness. Fortunately someone had seen us and alerted Hugh's father who came off in his boat to rescue us. Our boat was almost half full of water by the time he reached us. After all these years some of the details of that adventure are a bit hazy in my mind, but what I remember very clearly indeed is the skelped backside our rescuer gave each of us when he got us ashore.

Ronald Shearer, Sandwick.

At the Frotoft school entry to the classroom was through the boys' lobby. The girls' lobby was too small to play in, so on wet days when the teacher wanted no noise coming through to the schoolhouse at playtimes, we all played in the boys' lobby. There we would 'fleep the cat' on the corner pegs, and play ball games and blind man's buff. The girls' lobby held the cleaner's cupboard, a chipped enamel basin with soap and a jug of cold water. A door led to the courtyard and the girls' toilet which consisted of a seat and a bucket. The cleaner emptied the bucket every day on the midden in the corner of the playground. About the only other thing that went on the midden were the ashes from the fire.

Everybody walked to and from school except for a lucky few who had bikes. The children from Westness had 4 miles to walk every day. We used to shelter at various places from sleety showers, at 'the corner o the dyke' and under the brig being two of them. Our knees above our knee-length socks would be red and sore from the sleet, that is, when we weren't wearing those thick, brown, woollen stockings which granny knitted and which we loathed.

The only exams I can remember getting were the Qualifying and the Orkney and Shetland, after which some pupils went into the Kirkwall school, the girls living in part of the old Post Office hostel and the boys in digs. We managed home most weekends and many a rough crossing we had in Tom Sinclair's small motor boat. However bad it was, if Tom went it was safe to go, but often having to shelter under a big tarpaulin or up under the covered bow of the boat.

Rhoda Stevenson, Stronsay.

At the Sourin school, Mr. Wallace used to teach the older boys handwork while we girls were through in the junior room doing needlework. One day, near the end of term, when we returned to the senior room, Mr. Wallace showed us some of the articles the boys had made that term. There was an impressive array of tin mugs, toasting forks, and biscuit cutters. He then suggested that we should show the boys what we had been making at needlework, and indicated that I should lead the way by holding up my handiwork. I declined, and went on declining, despite the teacher's repeated requests and increasing annoyance. This act of defiance earned me the punishment of being kept in at 4 o'clock to write out lines.

What I had made at needlework was a pair of knickers for myself, and it would have been just too embarrassing for me to hold them up for the boys to giggle at.

Ann Wood, Evie.

I was seven when I came to the Wester school from Shapinsay. Lily Miller was the teacher at that time and there were very few pupils. A photograph, taken in 1947, shows only eight of us and Lily. I have very few memories of that part of my school life. Two that come to mind are of mixing cocoa and sugar in preparation for dinnertime, and of Anita of Ivybank doing an amazing number of skips in a competition at the picnic. Another memory is of watching from the playground as my grandfather's funeral procession made its way down from Furse to the kirkyard beside the loch.

Freda Murray, Moffat.

The view looking west from the Frotoft school is truly beautiful. The land from the top of Mansie Bichan's falls in terraces down to the sea. Further west, Eynhallow closes the far end of Evie Sound apart from Burger Roost on the south side and Whale Roost on the north. Then looking across the Sound, one has an open view of Costa, Evie, and Rendall right up to Gairsay and parts of the outer North Isles, and of course, part of Wyre. With a full westerly gale striking the high west side of Eynhallow, one could see the spume rising high into the air.

One wall of the classroom had a 2 ft. width of linoleum running its full length. In our early days at school we could stand there drawing with coloured chalks. That was before we graduated to crayons and later still, to water colours. I seem to remember that at each end of the room there was a row of regularly spaced holes drilled in the floor. What their function was I do not know. Perhaps they had something to do with ventilation, or with draining the water after floor washing. I can remember a family of mice taking up residence under the floor. No doubt, there were plenty of crumbs to attract them. Silence reigned in the classroom whenever they appeared one by one. Eventually, they all paid the price in cheese-laden traps.

On a wet morning, children from the Brinian and Westness would arrive at school pretty well sodden after their long trail. There was none of the good protective clothing that is available today. The smell of wet clothing drying around the classroom stove was never very pleasant. There must have been days when we went home still damp.

Who could ever forget the beautiful maps by Bartholomew and A.K. Johnston of Edinburgh that hung on the walls? There were also posters. One that I remember was of Indian children, scantily clad, playing under a palm tree. It bore the caption, 'Our dusky cousins at play.' Our history books told us of wonderful battles and glorious British victories in various parts of the world, and the myriad parts of the Empire, coloured in red, were pointed out to us on the maps. It was much later in life that we realised the amount of propaganda that had been fed to us.

Miss Mary Ann Sinclair was my teacher all the time I was at Frotoft and I am sure she was a good teacher. I have often thought that a one-teacher school must place very heavy demands upon the teacher. To divide the time in any working day amongst several classes, and giving a fair allocation of attention to the bright and not so bright pupils requires a great deal of skill and patience. Mary Ann coped rather well. She soon spotted the shirkers, and whether the repeated request of 'Please Miss, may I get out?' was genuine or not. Sometimes she got it wrong and the result appeared on the floor.

The school roll could fluctuate quite a lot depending on the movement of married farm servants at the large farms of Westness and Trumland at the term times in May and November. There was also frequently a bit of movement among the gamekeepers and gardeners at Trumland House and Westness House.

Near the end of a school day, Mary Ann would produce McDougall's mental arithmetic cards which I hated. The first pupil to give the correct answer to a question could pick up his/her schoolbag and scamper. I am afraid that I was seldom first away. I could get the answer but usually too slowly. Some would be half way home before I got out.

Writing on slates was never to my liking. A whole day's work could be erased with one sweep of the elbow if you were at odds with your deskmate. If you were unlucky enough to get a very hard slate pencil, it could be very annoying. To some it was a gift as they could bring out of the slate the most excruciating screeching in several different tones. Mary Ann did not have an ear for such sounds and knew how to deal with those who produced them. I liked the copperplate style of writing in our copy books. I can recall that two of the copybook lines we had to reproduce in our best hand were, 'Punctuality is the Principality of Princes' and 'Necessity is the Mother of Invention.'

The time of the summer Picnic and Sports was a great time to be at school. A time of fun and good things to eat. Mrs. Walter Grant of Trumland House always sent over a large tin of assorted biscuits and a box of chocolate bars for the children. Magic was the only word for that day. I seem to remember that old Mansie of Pliverha used to walk over from Wester with his fiddle to play at the dance with Harry Logie vamping on the piano. After the dance Mansie would have to face a long road home. We had more musicians when the Johnstons came to Trumland Farm as both father and son were good fiddle players.

My last two years at school were spent at Sourin where Miss Isabel Craigie was the teacher. She was a really excellent teacher and I made reasonably good progress in her class. I enjoyed the extra subjects we got, Latin and Chemistry. She had that something — I don't know what word or phrase sums it up — that made learning enjoyable. Perhaps she was born to impart knowledge in a manner that made any subject interesting. I can truthfully say that the day I heard that she had passed away filled me with sadness.

Jim Marwick, Kirkwall.

This story is not about school but about something that happened when I was six or seven years old, and is still talked about in our family today. One misty spring evening, my elder sister, Clara, and I had gone out over the braes to look for teeo eggs. Our little brother, Willie, who was four at the time, followed us, and when we discovered this, Clara turned back with him. She took him almost to the house and then left him to make his way in by himself. However, he did not go inside, but wandered off and got lost in the mist. Some time passed before it was realised that he was missing. A frantic search was made but there was no sign of him anywhere. Daylight was running out by that time, so neighbours were hastily alerted and men with lanterns came from all over the district to join in the search which went on all through the night, with no trace of Willie being found.

Shortly after first light, Peemo Clouston noticed from some distance that something in one of Quoyostray's ploughed fields was attracting his dog's attention. When he investigated he found Willie lying in the furrows, just waking up from a sleep. Fortunately, his night out in the open had not done him any great harm.

Clem Manson, Rousay.

I was at the Wasbister school in the 1940's. One winter there was very deep snow and some of the older children built an igloo. I was allowed into it only once or twice. It was surely quite an impressive structure for I remember several adults coming along to see it. In the long snow of 1947 we spent every playtime sledging on the road in front of the school. At first there was only one sledge but more soon appeared and with three on every sledge we all got sledging all the time.

Here are some playground rhymes we used to recite, usually in connection with some game we were playing:

> Eetle ottle black bottle
> Eetle ottle out.
> Tea and sugar is my delight
> Tea and sugar out.
>
> Henry Noddy, peedie body
> Ca'ed his tae in a curly-doddy.
> Up he got and doon he fell
> And ca'ed his tae in a tattie bell.

Counting on a child's fingers:

> This one broke the barn door,
> This one stealed the corn,
> This one ran awa,
> This one telt on a'.
> And peedie winkie stuck in the gutter
> And paid for it a'.

There must have been a concert every year, I think. Over the years the variety of acts did not change much. I remember Highland, Irish and even Hungarian dancing being done. One year the boys appeared in kilts doing either the Highland Fling or the Sword Dance. During December there was nothing but 'concert' in our minds and we really did our best to learn our parts. Some were good singers and even sang solo. Being tone deaf, I was not one of them. I can recall on one occasion being told by one of the bigger boys not to sing so loudly, and was much put out. The highlights of the concerts for us were when the adults put on an item or two. I can still remember Annabella o' Tou doing that 'Bake and Brew' sketch.

When I started school in 1943 we used slates but the older ones were mainly using paper and pencils. At first we used chalk on the slates but soon got on to slate pencils — lovely thin, smooth pencils they were, half covered in paper. When supplies of them ran out during the war, we were given thicker, harder ones which scratched the slates. Then one of the boys, Irvine Donaldson, I think it was, discovered a type of soft stone in the burn of Vacquoy that worked beautifully and did not scratch the slates. That summer it was a great craze to go looking for that special kind of stone. Once we had learned our letters we started using copy books but they went out of use during my time at school.

For most of my time at school I was in a class of one, so I freqently got taught along with the class above me. This was fine most of the time but there were two things I failed to pick up along the way. One was L.C.M., G.C.M. and factors and the other was analysis of sentences into their appropriate clauses.

The only prizes given out in my time were for attendance. I think I only ever got one for I was aye off with one thing or another. My sister, who was 'skinny' and was always being packed full of vitamins and malt, never took anything and ended up with more books.

Anita Thomson, Sanday.

When I started at Frotoft school there were only six other children. One, Ronald Stevenson, left after three months and another, Dave Gibson, after six. Dave's sister, Kathleen was the teacher throughout my time at school. She became Mrs. Harcus when I was 12. As the oldest pupil at that time it fell to me to present her with the wedding gift from the pupils. She cycled over from Hullion every morning and we would watch as she went past the window trying to judge by her expression what kind of mood she was in.

The day always started with the Lord's prayer followed by copybook time using pen and ink. We had a cup of cocoa at peedie playtime and kept our piece for the longer break. Playtime games included rounders, football and picko. On wet days we played marbles and 'Pussy wants a corner' in the boys' lobby.

The teacher's desk had two compartments which we never got the chance of looking into. We knew the strap was kept in one of them for it was frequently brought out and used. Sometimes it was left on the desktop to act as a warning. Another thing that was kept in the desk was a set of mental arithmetic cards. The teacher sometimes took us out to the floor and asked us questions from these cards. The strap would have been preferable!

The highlight of the school year was the picnic held at the end of June. Everybody in the district attended, old and young. I cannot remember a picnic day when the sun did not shine. The grown-ups enjoyed watching the children's races, and some of the youngsters' fun came from watching their elders making fools of themselves at the wheelbarrow, sack, and thread-the-needle races. The dance that always followed the picnic was always a lively affair with all ages joining in. The old ladies would enjoy watching the latest romance and who was dancing with whom, and how often. Dresses old and new would be commented on. Supper was served as darkness fell and the oil lamps were lit.

The school cleaner had the task of emptying the bucket from the girls' toilet several times during the evening and from time to time she sent me out to take a look and report back if it was time for another trip to the midden.

Sheila Lyon, Sandwick.

The most daunting task I had to face when I started school was just getting there, for from Scockness that meant a two mile trek. Having to do that on a cold, wet, wintery morning in the teeth of a westerly gale was not something for a five year-old to look forward to. On reaching the brae of Pow on a really wild morning we sometimes got a lift from Hugh o' Pow who would be taking Annabella to school in the cart. Never was a hurl in a cart more welcome despite having to huddle under empty grain sacks to keep the rain off.

The bigger of the two rooms at the Sourin school had a large stove that was a great comfort on cold days. It stood 18 inches or so out from the wall with a thick metal stovepipe going horizontally into the wall and chimney. I remember a tall boy, who is now one of Sourin's senior citizens, sitting astride that pipe to dry off wet trousers. The seat was burnt out of his trousers by the time he realised something was amiss, and he had to beat a hasty retreat homewards for another pair.

I had not been at school long when six big boys from Wasbister began attending at Sourin. To me as a peedie boy they appeared very mature and grown-up. When ever there was sufficient frost or snow we would create slides, and even in the tackety boots we wore we could get up to a fair speed on these slides. One of the Wester boys made us all feel envious when he turned up with a pair of home made skates which were iron shod. Two of these Wester boys played truant on one occasion and spent the whole day in the Leean. On another occasion one of that pair turned up at school on his father's light-weight motor bike. Motor bikes were few and far between at that time and of great interest to us boys. No wonder we regarded him as quite a hero.

My first teacher was Miss Rendall, a kindly person who was getting on in years and finding a few unruly boys a bit difficult to cope with. She wisely decided to move to Egilsay for her final few years in teaching. She was followed by Miss Harper for a short time and then Ruby Brown came. She encouraged us to read books and write good essays. There were no specialist teachers visiting the isles then as there are now. A teacher of the calibre of Miss Craigie could handle all these subjects herself. She was a good pianist and a beautiful singer so music was no problem. She was a good all round teacher, a wise and kindly person who could discipline fairly, and one who earned respect naturally.

Jackie Wallace taught us to solder syrup tins into mugs and fencing wire into toasting forks. The handwork he gave us was both interesting and useful. He taught the boys how to splice rope and quite a few well made halters were taken home to the farms. In his cookery class for boys there were plenty of volunteers to sample our chips but none for our porridge. He also taught us some much needed football skills, and to such good effect that we had an easy victory when we took on a joint Wester/Frotid team.

I can recall some enjoyable performances at school concerts — a boy and a girl giving a touching rendition of 'Where are you going to my pretty maid?' — another pair dancing the Sailor's Hornpipe, and looking the part in square rig — John Grieve, Billy Mainland, John Seatter and I harmonising on shepherd's reeds.

There are two old Sourin worthies that I associate with my early schooldays. One was old Jeemie Grieve o' Ooterdykes who used to come down to the Co-op or the mill with his ox drawn cart. He had a disability which forced him to prop up his chin with his fist. The other old worthy was Macom o' Faro, a Moses-like figure with a long, white beard, and having a temper that kept us children at a safe distance. He faithfully tended the kirkyard at Scockness, wheeling his tools down in a barrow and doing the cutting with a scythe or sometimes a huick. The grass was carefully gathered up and wheeled home to Faro for his cow. If there was no grass his load would be ware from the shore at Ham to fertilise his few acres.

One more memory, of my latter days at Sourin — of 'asking out' from the senior room and making eyes at a certain girl as I passed through the junior room — of being pounced on by Ruby Brown who fairly enjoyed the situation — and of my red-faced embarrassment.

George Craigie, Glencarse, Perth.

I enjoyed my time at school in Wasbister. The only thing I didn't like was grammar. Miss Norquoy was the teacher when we started on grammar and I just could not understand it and that used to worry me. Then Miss Taylor came and she explained it in a way I could understand. After that I got on fine. We got an awful lot of arithmetic, especially when the Clerk was taking the school. With him we seemed to do arithmetic all day.

I remember that one day a story went round the district that a motor bike was coming to the island that day, the first motor bike in Rousay. We waited on tenterhooks all day for this motor bike to come by the school but there was no sign of it. A lot of us from Furse, Sketquoy, and Hammerfield were on our way home when we saw it coming down the brae above Quoyostray. In sheer panic we climbed the dyke of Kuiv and went tearing across the field to get out of the way of the approaching monster. I cannot now remember what it was we saw but it turned out not to be the motor bike after all.

Annabella Clouston, aged 90, Rousay.

It is almost sixty years since I left the Sourin school. At the start of my time there Miss Baikie was the teacher but I had her for only six months before she left to get married and to be replaced by Miss Rendall. Later on we had Miss Harper and Miss Brown.

I had a long distance to walk from Scockness to the school. I can remember being very afraid to pass a certain field that had a bull in it, even though there was a dyke between us. A very busy place we had to pass was the meal mill where there was often a collection of horses and carts to be seen. We had to take care not to be soaked by the water splashing off the millwheel.

I remember Miss Craigie's arrival. I have heard her described as a born teacher and I think it was true. She took the two top classes and during her time in Sourin she taught two boys who were to be dux medallists at Kirkwall Grammar School. They were David Marwick and Tom Walls.

I had a happy time at school and wish the school at Sourin every success in future.

Ann M. Alexander, Glencarse, Perth.

All through my school days I got the strap only once. At the Wester (Wasbister) school we all had a small bottle of water and a cloth for cleaning our slates with. Well, one day I was sitting in the seat in front of George Sinclair and I turned round and poured his bottle of water over his slate of sums. I suppose it washed them all away. The teacher was very cross with me and gave me nine pages of geography to learn at home that night. That was an awful lot of geography to take in in one night so little wonder that I could not answer the teacher's questions on it the next day. That was why I got the strap. I thought it would have been fairer to have been given it for the original offence.

I was five years old when my father took very ill and had to go to hospital. A horse-drawn ambulance came out on the steamer and halfway round the island to pick him up. I can remember watching from the playground and seeing that ambulance going up the road towards the pier. I was never to see him again.

A happier memory is of the first Christmas party I remember at school. Maybe I was not even school age at the time for all the bairns in the district were included in the fun. We were all up to high doh waitng for Santa to appear. One of the grown-ups came in and announced that Santa would soon be there, as he had seen his sledge coming down over Innister. Innister — to think that Santa was coming down over my own house — oh what excitement. Then a commotion in the lobby, and there he was, standing in the doorway, an old man with snow-white whiskers and wearing a brilliant red coat, and with a bulging sack on his back. I can still remember how thrilled I was by it all.

Phebe Lennie, Orphir.

My first teacher at Sourin was Miss Baikie and when she left to marry Willie Corsie, Miss Rendall arrived. She was very kind to the children and some may have been inclined to take advantage. I seem to remember that I was one of those who gave her a hard time of it.

The bare wooden boards of the floor were well worn with the tackety boots we wore and the knots were left sticking up.

I can mind learning some of the alphabet before I started school by attaching to each letter the name of someone I knew. So it was A for Albert (my uncle), B for Bella (of Whiteha'), C for Chrissie (my sister), and D for Davina (my granny). That is why I had no bother learning my letters when I went to school.

I remember going on a picnic to Trumland House. Some of the bigger boys got a ride in a car there which had a fold down roof like the hood of a pram. It must have been one of the first cars in Rousay. One of the first motor bikes I saw belonged to Dr. Thomson. When we saw him coming along the road towards the school we all ran to the playground dyke to see him going by in a cloud of dust.

Something that I remember well from my schooldays was Willie o' Digro and me catching six sea trout in the burn down at the mill. They were so long that the skin was off their tails before we got them home. The only thing I got a really good hiding for, along with some others, was for trying to see who could pee the highest up the wall. Another time was for not learning a piece from 'The Lay of the Last Minstrel.' That was in Frank Kent's time. He used to call the strap the leather medicine.

Hughie Russell, Kirkwall.

I remember one winter when I was about eleven (over 50 years ago), two or three of us decided to roast tatties in the oven of the classroom stove. The teacher knew nothing about this, of course. We reckoned that if we put in the tatties at peedie playtime when the teacher went round to the schoolhouse for her morning tea, they should be roasted by big playtime at one o'clock. We each took twa three tatties and the plan worked fine. Only once did we fear we were going to be found out, when the teacher remarked that that there was a peculiar smell coming from the fire. However, she never found out what it was.

I remember the Co-op manager coming to the door one day and having a hurried conversation with the teacher. She then marched us out to the end of the shop where we could get a good view of the meal mill which was on fire with flames shooting out of the roof. We wanted to go closer, but no, back to our desks and our lessons.

I had a mile or so to walk to school over rough, muddy cart tracks and across burns and ditches that were often so full after heavy rain that I had to get across on the handrail to keep out of the water that would be up over the bridge. I think of those days, and then I think of our grand-daughter today who hardly ever walks the short distance to her school. She just takes it for granted that she will be driven to and fro in the car!

Thelma Leslie, Holm.

Miss Baikie was the teacher when I was at the Sourin school. There were two others in my class, Samuel Inkster of Woo and George Corsie of Knarston. Mrs. Mary Mainland of Gorehouse was our sewing mistress and I still have a lovely little silver brooch that I won as a sewing prize all those years ago. I cannot remember ever using jotters. We had slates all the time at school. They had wooden frames and were ruled on one side. I can remember that I was very fond of drawing and painting buttercups.

The picnic was held at Faraclett. The food and other essentials were carried in a cart and we all followed on behind, each of us carrying a small Union Jack flag. A day of fun and races, and cookies with strawberry jam.

Hugh Marwick of Guidhall (Dr. Hugh's father) was Attendance Officer at that time. When he visited the school he called out our names from the register and we had to answer, 'Here, sir.'

Harrold's van, with Sammy Inkster in charge, was sometimes passing the school as we left for home and Sammy would lighten our homeward trudge by letting us put our schoolbags in the van.

Sally Marwick, Rousay.

I well remember my first day at Sourin School. I was very annoyed that my mother insisted on coming with me as I thought I was big enough to manage myself. In the course of the day I had a fight with Robert Seatter on the flag floor of the boys' porch at the school. The day ended with some more commotion when John Inkster of Woo, who used to do some carting for the Co-op next door to the school, broke his leg in an accident.

When I was at school, my father had not long taken over Scockness and I knew from an early age that a future in farming awaited me. That suited me fine as it was my only interest. I used to watch the horse ploughs slowly converting the stubble fields into dark furrowed rigs and longed for the day I could leave school. I learned to plough at an early age, taught mostly by John Craigie of Breck who had great patience with me. I still had not reached the leaving age of 14 when I competed in my first ploughing match, for I had to ask for a day off school to take part. It was held at Westness that year, I mind, on a very stormy January day. My dad took a bit of persuading before agreeing to set off on the long road round to Westness on such a wild morning. My ploughing did not win me a prize that day but I got one for being the youngest ploughman. Being called a ploughman was honour enough for me.

Our main teacher was Isabel Craigie. We were all very fond of her and I think she did a good job. I remember one weekend when she had given all the boys in my class lines to do but we knew she would not be there on the Monday as she was going home to Shetland to see her mother who was ill. So of course we did not bother doing the lines. We got a rude surprise when we turned up at school and found Frank Kent in charge for the week. What was worse was that he must have been told about the lines so we ended up getting a strapping we never forgot.

A few years before I left school, new science tables arrived so for the last two years I was there we got Science, Latin, Algebra and Geometry as well as the usual subjects. That was when the older pupils from Wasbister and Frotoft started coming to Sourin.

We used to be sent out in pairs to collect money for some good cause or other. Two of us would be given all the small places above the school, over past the manse , and on as far as Grips. The usual amount given was a shilling (5p), and sixpence (2½p) from pensioners, and if you got the odd half-crown that was big money. When I think back on that, I feel proud of these people who in many cases had very little to give, but we were never turned away.

Hugh Craigie, Ballater.

My memories of schooldays are mostly of hard work, fear of the teacher, and very little in the way of diversions. I remember that there were only four occasions in the year when lessons were set aside, a walk up the burn in the spring, the picnic in summer, Hallowe'en, and Christmas when a concert was held. A year passed very slowly.

We walked to school in all kinds of weather and warmed ourselves around the old black stove. During the winter months, we all brought cocoa, sugar and milk. The teacher boiled a kettle of water at lunchtime and she always did the pouring out. Come summer, we sat under the playground dyke in the sun eating our jammy pieces and drinking the small bottles of milk which we brought from home. It tasted good and we were hungry!

I can well remember sitting outside and hearing German planes flying overhead in the early stages of the second world war. Their engines had a very pronounced thud and were easily recognised. We frequently saw them high in the sky, and usually three at a time. The dangers of war were not brought home to us until the first bombing raid over Orkney in which our teacher's brother-in-law was killed. That really made us think what war meant and, as he was the first fatality, in our little minds Orkney was famous.

The Spring walk, usually up the burn of Vacquoy, was a welcome change. We looked for birds' nests, fished for brandies, and admired the foxgloves, wild roses and other flowers growing along the banks. The waterfall, up near Turbitail, was the turning point. It was only a few feet high and had a pool at the bottom, but to us it was a great sight. On the return journey we picked primroses and I can remember the school window sills overflowing with them.

The next highlight of the year was the picnic. This meant new plimsolls and practising the races beforehand. The faster you ran the more pennies you collected on the day.

Hallowe'en was celebrated by dooking for apples in a big tub. We also had apples hanging by strings from the ceiling. Standing with hands behind our backs and trying to get a bite at the swinging apple was no easy task. The fact that the first to do so were two runny-nosed boys in our midst was rather off-putting but the thought of being the only child not to get an apple was enough to overcome my qualms and urged me to have a go!

Early December found us rehearsing for the Christmas concert. Decorations and balloons lined the school walls. The platform surrounded by curtains was set up at one end of the room leaving a very small assemby area for the children. If any dressing up was involved, this was done in the schoolhouse which we reached by climbing through a handy window beside the stage. This was great fun but it had to be done very quietly. No giggling allowed. When the concert was over we waited impatiently for the knock on the door that would announce Santa's arrival. I can recall that on one occasion, a rather jovial Santa came in, grabbed our teacher and gave her a big hug and a kiss. She, being a middle aged spinster, was very embarrassed and not at all amused, but we onlookers thought it was hilarious.

Evelyn Marwick, Rousay.

I started school in Sourin in February, 1926. My mother says that I went willingly enough but when I came home I said school wasn't a fine place and I was not going back. It was a one teacher school at that time with Miss Rendall as the teacher. I remember we learned to read from thin, red covered books which had lists of words at the tops of the pages. Starting with words like at, bat, cat, hat, etc., we said the letters individually followed by the word. I don't know how we managed to learn because, when I later became a teacher myself, I found phonetics, sounding the letters, much easier to teach. We did sums from an Alexander sum book and by Primary 3 we were doing addition sums with three figures across and six or seven rows down. I loathed the copy books in which we used to practise our writing. Each line we wrote seemed to get worse and worse.

I had not been long at school when Miss Craigie M.A. arrived to teach the senior classes. The smaller classroom, which had been empty until then, had the floor stepped up towards the back. This was lowered to one level and a sink was installed. Two large science tables arrived along with all the equipment and chemicals needed for science lessons. Miss Rendall could not stand the smells that emanated from the other classroom on science days. She told us they reminded her of her stay in hospital some time previously.

Miss Craigie taught the Advanced Division which soon attracted six boys from Wasbister. They seemed so big to us. The qualifying exam for the Advanced Division consisted of papers in English, Arithmetic, History and Geography. After that, our school day began at 9.30 instead of 10 as it was for the junior classes. We then had science, algebra, and geometry extra, and any pupils intending to go on to school in Kirkwall stayed in after school and had Latin lessons. When Tom Walls and I went to Kirkwall in 1934 we were ahead of our contemporaries in the Grammar School in all subjects except French which we hadn't been taught in Rousay. We had to stay in after school then to catch up in our French.

The inspector who came to the school was an old, small, fat man. Miss Rendall used to get very worked up as the time for his visit approached and this affected us in the same way. Dr. Bannerman arrived annually for the medical inspections. We didn't like him much either for, I suppose, we were a bit shy about taking off our jumpers at school.

On Mondays there was never any bread left for our school pieces so we were given a penny at home, and at playtime we waited expectantly for the Co-op cart to arrive from the pier with the boxes of still-warm bread. Our penny bought us two cookies and how delicious they were!

Kathie Stockan, Sandwick.

I started school from Falquoy. I must have been very frightened because I howled a lot, as I recall. Miss Annie Craigie was my first teacher but only for a short time till she married and went to Canada. Miss Mathieson was there for the rest of my time at school.

I hated using slates but we did not seem to have them for long and soon moved on to jotters. Having learned to read, I found an exciting, new world opening up for me. It was pure joy. When we had school concerts I would write out a complete play and form it into a little book. I still have some of these but I find it somewhat painful to look them over now. It's so long ago.

The approach of Christmas at school found us learning our parts for the concert held at that time. I remember once, as a very small girl dressed as a fairy, having to open a concert. I wore a very short muslin dress made by my mother and I carried a tinsel wand with a star on top. She covered my carpet slippers with white satin and glued the satin on to the soles with egg-white, and trimmed them with tinsel. With my hair tinselled as well, I must have sparkled for once! I often think how clever and innovative my mother must have been.

In the summer months we took a HP bottle filled wth milk to school to help wash down our playtime pieces as we sat under the dyke in the sunshine. Sometimes we would leave an inch or two of milk in the bottle which, after some vigorous shaking, would turn to butter.

Cathleen Craigie, Rousay.

I had a short spell at the Wester school under Tina Mathieson before we moved to Sandwick for a few years. The only school memory I have of that time is of Francis and I and John from Braehead, on the way home one day, walking the whole length of the park of Tou in the ditch under the snow that had fanned up over the dyke. I can remember being severely told off when we got home because we were ever so slightly wet! I can just mind what must have been my first school concert. I had to recite a poem, the title of which I now forget, but the opening line was, 'I wish I had a little dog, its tail up in the air.'

Miss Sutherland was the teacher when we returned to Wester. Then, during the war we had Mrs. Goar. She had farming connections so when she was there we had no trouble getting out of school to work in the harvest or to lift tatties. I don't think she could have had a radio as we used to tell her news about the war. Maybe she classed this as a form of history lesson but it was better than doing sums and some days we would keep it going till playtime. I'm quite sure that half of what we told her was a lot of rubbish. I also remember her Christmas concerts. For one of them she taught us to dance the eightsome reel, and for the week before the concert Peemo of Tou used to come down and provide the music for us on the fiddle. He must have had many a laugh at us.

Our next teacher was Lily Miller who was a better teacher in every way. She was young, and keen to do well. The results from the school must have shown a marked improvement during her time there. I sat the Orkney and Zetland exam, both the junior and senior sections. I can remember working up to the senior one for what seemed months, but probably wasn't that long. All the others were given a holiday while I had to sit the exam on my own with Mark Kirkness there to supervise. I must have passed because I remember seeing my name in the Orcadian along with all the others from other schools.

In winter there was not very much heat in the school in the mornings. With certain airts of wind the fire would not vent and we either had to sit and be kippered in the smoke and soot or else the fire was allowed to go out and we sat in the cold. If this happened on very cold days we were sent home, so it was not unknown for lots of coal to be piled on during playtime in the hope that we would be sent home. Sometimes it worked but sometimes it didn't and we just had to put up with the consequences of our misdeeds.

Neil Craigie, Stromness.

After leaving the Sourin school I worked on a nearby croft. One day I was working near the loch of Quoys which is only about 100 yards from the school and some boys were also there. Along came Jock Leonard from Quoys taking his mare for a drink. Jock was an exceptionally small man, very little over 4 feet, I would think. He was known to one and all as Ticken, but no-one who knew of his fierce temper dared to call him that to his face. This was not known to the youngest boy in the group, Archer Clouston, who had never heard Jock called anything but Ticken. In all innocence he turned to Jock and asked, 'Whit dis thoo ca thee mare, Ticken?' As soon as they heard the question, the other boys took to their heels but Archer, being a quick learner, was not far behind, spurred on, no doubt, by the roars of rage coming from the wee man.

Roy Russell, Holm.

My schooldays started during the First War when Miss Hourston was the teacher at Frotoft. Miss Anna May Cooper came after her for a short time till Mary Ann Sinclair took over. I mind a very heavy snow in 1918 during Miss Cooper's time. She stayed with relatives in Wester and the snow was so deep that she couldn't get around to Frotoft, so the school was closed for three weeks because of it.

In the springtime, Miss Sinclair sometimes allowed us to burn heather up behind the school where there was no danger of the fire spreading. One day when it came near time for her to call us back in at the end of dinnertime, some of us hid in the smoke where she could not see us. We knew fine she would not come into to it looking for us. That put an end to the heather burning.

James Smith, Kirkwall.

For most of my time at the Wasbister school we sat at long desks holding six or eight of us but they had all been replaced by the two-seater type before I left. The bare wooden floor was washed and scrubbed with disinfectant each weekend. Healthier, I think, than the carpets in today's school.

We took a piece to school with us which consisted of loaf and jam, or oat-cakes and cheese, and sometimes just bere bannocks and treacle. By play-time the treacle had all seeped into the bread but it tasted all right when you were hungry. In the summertime when the milk was plentiful we took a HP bottle of milk to school and drank it to wash down our piece. In winter the teacher boiled a kettle of water as big playtime approached and we all had a cup of hot cocoa. Each family kept a tin at school filled with a mixture of cocoa and sugar. The milk for the cocoa was brought daily in a small bottle.

We used to dread the visits of Dr. Bannerman. He had such an abrupt manner. He always had a big, brown dog with him that none of us trusted. Summers seemed to be far better then than they are now. There were weeks of summer dresses and bare feet and the sun shining every day. We were all hardier then than the bairns now. They have so many sick turns and colds, and always something going the rounds in the school. I wonder if all this carpeting and central heating is a bit overdone.

In my 9 years of schooling I never missed an attendance. The Education Committee used to give a watch to any pupil who achieved this but they had stopped doing so by the time I left. However the teacher, Miss Mathieson, bought a watch for me out of her own pocket and it was presented to me at the last picnic I attended as a pupil. Years later I was to marry someone who had won a watch for the same achievement at the Wyre school.

Clara Craigie, Dounby

I was a pupil at Frotoft school from 1952 till it closed in 1960. I then moved to the new school in Sourin for my last year of Primary schooling. What a change that was for us! Flush toilets instead of dry closets, bright, cheerful, warm classrooms, school dinners and a huge hall in which to eat them, and electric lights were some of the things that were new to us. Over at the Co-op we could buy a packet of crisps, a snowball and a penny chew for 6d ($2^1/_2$p). I can remember the visits of the dentist to the school. Everybody's teeth needed attention because, living on an island, we weren't taken to the dentist often enough.

I suppose I should have liked the new school, with all its fine facilities, better than the old one at Frotoft, but I didn't. I always thought there was something very special about the Frotoft school. I still think that, and not just because it is now my home.

Olive Kemp, Rousay.

I started at the Sourin school in 1911 when Jessie Marwick of Guidal was the teacher. That was just a few months before she left to get married. Miss Baikie was my teacher for the rest of my schooldays.

In the summer months when eggs were plentiful, the Co-op shop used to pickle eggs which were then sold in the winter time when the prices were higher. Large wooden tubs were used for this and after use they were left to steep for a while in the nearby loch of Quoys. They were a great attraction for us boys, and great fun we had sailing around the loch in them. I remember one day we were all out in the boats when the teacher called us in. One boy, in his haste to reach the shore, fell overboard and crawled to the edge on all fours. He made for home but took care not to arrive there before the normal time. By that time his clothes would be dry enough not to betray him.

We used to play a chasing and catching game called come-a-lee, and another called rabbits which was similar to rounders. For our games of football we never had any ball other than a golf ball.

In my early days at school the Co-op shop was at Clumpy. On Tuesdays when the steamer came out with new bread we trooped up to Clumpy at playtime to buy fresh cookies.

In 1918 the Sourin burn overflowed its banks after a period of very heavy rain. The water was up over the brigs and reached as far as the crossroads.

Jeemie Grieve, Rousay.

I began school at Frotoft when Miss Sinclair was the teacher. I dearly loved her and truly, schooldays were happy days — no bullying in those times. Everyone seemed to be friendly, with the older children taking care of the little ones and all playing together happily.

Miss Sinclair seldom used the strap but I can well remember once when it had surely been used and not put back in her desk where it was kept. At playtime one of the older boys popped it behind a picture which hung on the wall. Nothing was ever said about it, but it was there till the walls were redecorated some months later. We all thought it really funny at the time.

Maisie Kirkness, Aberdeen.

Our family lived at Banks in Sourin when I was a boy and I went to the nearby school. One of my duties every morning was to deliver milk to the schoolhouse. I got tuppence a week from the teacher for doing this, and another tuppence came every Saturday from the Co-op manager for delivering his milk. I suppose that most of that money was spent on sweeties during the following week. The time came, however, during my later schooldays, when cigarettes held more appeal than sweeties. Tuppence could buy a packet of five Woodbines in the 1930s. A penny for a box of matches still left something for sweeties. Into the lavatories at playtimes to enjoy a few quick puffs shared with a friend or two. No fear of being caught by the teacher. She was in the schoolhouse enjoying a fag of her own with her eleven o'clock cup of tea.

John Seatter, Kirkwall.

The Co-op shop was next door to the school in Sourin, and all round that area was a happy hunting ground for us boys at playtimes especially when there was nothing better to do, such as playing football. It was there that one of the bigger boys might manage to buy a packet of five Woodbines which cost two old pence. When that happened clouds of smoke could be seen rising from the boys' lavatories at playtime. One fine summer's day I was over at the Co-op when John Craigie, who was the School Attendance Officer, arrived on his bike. 'Hid's a grand day,' I said by way of greeting. 'Aye,' came the reply, 'and you aal seem to be enjoyan hid. I see the p—hoose is on fire again.'

John Grieve, St. Ola.

I did not see very much of school after my mother died sixty years ago. I was only twelve years old at the time, the elder of two girls in the family. Times were hard in the 1930s and there was no money for my father to employ a housekeeper. It fell to me to take on the job of cooking and baking, washing and mending and all the other household tasks that my mother had done. I had also to look after the hens, an important source of income at that time. Another task was doing the milking. Relatives and neighbours taught me how to cook and bake and I knew that I could always turn to them for help and advice. And how badly I needed help and advice! Many a time I wished that my mother had lived just a little longer, so that I could have had the benefit of all that she would have taught me in my teens. I was off school a lot that year, especially during the busy times on the farm. When I reached my thirteenth birthday, my father got exemption from school for me, and I was at home from that time onwards.

Looking back on it now, I suppose it was a dreadfully heavy burden to place on the shoulders of a child of twelve, but I did not look at it like that at the time. I was the eldest girl, my sister being only nine, and I suppose that I simply thought it was my duty to do the best I could for the sake of the family.

Chrissie Seatter, Kirkwall.

My most vivid memory of life at school in Rousay comes from my last year at the Sourin school which I attended for three years. My teacher was a tall, burly man whom I reckoned at that time to have a temper to match his physique. When marking our completed work he would often get so angry that he would hurl a jotter across the classroom aiming at the pupil concerned. While showing us examples on the blackboard, and getting wrong answers to questions asked, he would throw the chalk. Although I was never personally at the receiving end of what I can only describe as outbursts of bad temper, I nevertheless developed a great inward fear of this man.

It was at this time that my mother decided that I should further my education at Kirkwall Grammar School when I reached 14. She approached my teacher and asked him if he would teach me Latin during my last year. He told her he could not fit this into his timetable but he was quite willing to give me half an hour's tuition after school hours from four to four-thirty. On looking back, I think this was very kind of him considering that he was gaining nothing for the extra work involved. The Latin lessons started and went well for a few weeks, but my fear of the man was growing rapidly. The classroom seemed to grow bigger after all the other children had gone home and I was left all alone with the teacher. After 4-5 weeks I knew I couldn't go on and that I would have to do something about it.

One day, at five to four, I gathered up enough courage to walk out to the teacher's table and tell him a little white lie. I said my mother had decided not to send me to Kirkwall after all so there was no need to continue with the Latin lessons. He looked surprised but didn't say much, other than that I could go with the others. My mother was none too pleased at my backing out, but then, she never knew the true reason for it.

Jean Marwick, Ballingry.

My memories are mainly of the Frotoft school where most of my schooldays were spent, though I did attend the Sourin school as well, for a short time.

The classroom had none of the bright colours seen in today's schools. Above the brown wooden dado the walls were distempered. One or two large maps hung on the walls, but little else, except a calendar. It was not customary to display any of the pupils' work on the walls at that time.

We used slates when I first went to school in 1945, but I seem to remember that we soon moved on to jotters. I do recall having a small bottle with a screw top, in which some holes had been punched, that held water for slate cleaning. Some of my most vivid memories are of the cast-iron range which was the only form of heating in the school. During the lunch hour, when we were unsupervised, we sometimes stoked the thing up with coal until it was virtually red-hot. But I have no recollection of anyone ever getting burnt. To think of such a potential disaster area fills me with horror today, though no-one seemed to give it much thought in those days. That old range was later replaced with a slightly less dangerous enamelled stove which was better enclosed and which burned anthracite.

A cupboard that stood in a corner had a large drawer at the bottom which held the sewing and knitting. The boys were taught knitting along with the girls. It can be argued that it did us boys no harm, though I cannot think of any way in which it furthered my career! I remember knitting a scarf which I suspect my mother still has, and a pair of slippers. I would not claim that either item was an outstanding example of craft work. I heard recently of a man who had been taught to knit when he was a boy at Wasbister School. He became such an accomplished performer on the needles that his daughters, throughout their schooldays, were always dressed in splendid jerseys that had been knitted by their dad.

Presumably there had been two teachers at Frotoft at one time as there was a second room which was used for storage in our time. This was always referred to as the classroom. It never seemed to occur to us that the room in which we were taught was a classroom.

The only washing facilities were in the girls' lobby where, under the window was a low, built-in cupboard, the top of which had a round hole holding an enamel basin. The original vanitary unit! Beside it stood a pail of water. The basin often stood with water in it because, in the absence of any drainage, it could only be thrown outside. The cupboard was large enough to hold even one of the older boys and was sometimes made use of when we were playing hide and seek. I remember one occasion when I was doing the seeking, finding an older boy hiding there. Without stopping to consider the consequences, I picked up the basin of dirty water and emptied it over him down through the hole. How far I got before he caught me, I can't remember, but I live to tell the tale.

A bag containing the cleaner's materials hung in one corner of the girls' lobby. It was in the bottom of this bag that we once hid a dead and very 'high' mole. A parent, visiting Aberdeenshire, had brought it home for our education, for most of us had never before seen such a creature. The source of the dreadful smell was pondered for several days but never ascertained because the offending corpse was removed again before it was discovered.

In the boys' lobby a hatch in the high ceiling gave access to the roof space. Underneath the hatch was a wall cupboard. By using its shelves as a ladder we could climb up and stand on the top of the door. From that position any of the bigger boys could stretch up to the hatch and pull himself up into the attic. The smaller boys could not stretch far enough so the only way they could sample the delights of attic exploration was by getting pulled up while standing in a loop made at the end of the long rope that was always kept at school for the girls to use at skipping. Fortunately this practice did not end in the sort of disaster that might have been expected, with a ten foot drop on to a flagstone floor. But end it most certainly did when the teacher came in unexpectedly to find one of the smaller boys dangling halfway between floor and ceiling. Was it the lack of challenging activities that made us do such things or was it simply a case of boys being boys?

One-teacher schools had many drawbacks, not least of which was that only super-human teachers could be good at teaching all subjects, and I certainly never came across one of them. The fact that I was taught mostly by women teachers may not wholly account for my being useless at sport, but I think it must have been a contributory factor. This must be borne out, to some extent, by the fact that none of my contemporaries excelled at sport either. Nor, to my knowledge, did any later product of Frotoft ever shine on the sports field.

Schooling in Rousay, at that time, did little to stimulate a child's imagination. History, which should have been an interesting subject, seemed only to require an ability to memorize dates, of battles etc., which meant little to us. Yet we lived in an area that was richer in history than most other places we could think of. Admittedly, not all of it had been written about at that time, but I find it hard to believe that we could not have been taught something about the First World War, Scapa Flow, and the German Fleet, not to mention the ancient history of Orkney, especially in a place like Rousay that has such a wealth of archaelogical sites.

Perhaps one thing that did a little to stimulate our imaginations was the annual Christmas concert. In the little plays, in which we acted, we became different characters for a short time. The week leading up to the concert was a happy time with normal lessons being suspended and the time devoted to practising our turns.

When we decided to have a change of sporting activity we hit on the idea of playing cricket, quite undaunted by the fact that we had no cricket bat. We soon found that the shovel from the coal bucket made a satisfactory substitute. Sometimes we went bathing down at the beach below Hunclet at playtime. Drying ourselves was a bit of a problem because there was only one hand towel at the school at any one time and it was sopping wet after the first one had dried himself. Tough luck if you happened to be third or fourth in line.

Ian Craigie, Skye.

I got all my schooling at the Frotoft school. I had three teachers, Mrs. Harcus, Miss Sinclair, and Mrs. Grieve. In between two of them we had a student teaching us for a fortnight, Some days about a quarter to four he would give each of the classes a little competition or puzzle and as soon as you got the right answer you got away home. I was in the top class by that time and he asked us to write down a word having at least ten letters. We could not use dictionaries or other books, and the spelling had to be right. I remembered that we had the word 'accommodation' in our reading lesson that morning but I couldn't remember how to spell it. I asked out for a drink of water and while outside took a quick look at a card which hung in the window facing outwards. It gave the dimensions of the classroom and the number of children it could hold. Across the top of it was the word I wanted. When I returned to the classroom I wrote down ACCOMMODATION and was the first out of school that day, feeling very pleased with myself.

Mattie Grieve, Dounby.

To experience the welcome of a bright, stimulating classroom nowadays makes me realise how drab, bare and high-windowed was the schoolroom in Wasbister where I started my education in 1950.

In one corner of the room was a pile of long wooden forms for use at evening functions. During my first few days at school I chose to lie on these and 'write' on my slate. I considered this position preferable to occupying one of the long, high-backed desks. The teacher thought otherwise, and neither did she approve when I addressed her by her first name despite previous warnings about this at home.

In my imagination I can still taste and smell those slate pencils as I laboured with the basics of writing and numbers. Who could have even imagined that 40 years on, five year olds would be using such sophisticated machines as word processors?

I still remember my first Radiant Way reading books with their contrived emphasis on phonics. Having mastered the mechanics of reading, I encountered a dearth of suitable reading material. How wonderful it would have been if the rich array of inviting books found in today's classrooms had been available to us in those days before television.

I thought that a great advance had been made when the school acquired a radio and we could listen to some of the special broadcasts for schools. 'Music and Movement' was one of my favourites. I recall the pleasure I felt in producing jotters full of sums and pages of mostly copied sentences in our best cursive writing. There was also the competitive thrill of comprehension exercises, spelling tests, and dictation. In contrast to the creativity that is encouraged today, there was disappointment in our essays, paintings and drawings which never seemed to be quite perfect enough.

My days at Wasbister school passed happily, interspersed with holidays that (so my memory tells me) went on for ever in weather that was nothing short of idyllic! However, the Qualifying Examination loomed, accompanied by intriguing talk of the opportunities that would open up to those who passed well enough to proceed to secondary education at Kirkwall.

My island schooling had served me well and, with trepidation, I enrolled at Kirkwall Grammar School in 1957. This was a very big step into the unknown for a child that had rarely been out of the district let alone out of the island, and who would be allowed home only at holiday times. This restriction soon ended and we got home most weekends.

Whenever I wearied of my new life, and I often did in the early days, I was reminded that conditions had been considerably harder for earlier generations of isles' pupils at Kirkwall, and that I should be grateful. I was, and I am.

Sheena Marwick, Rousay.

When I was young the highlight of the year was the School Picnic. The Wasbister one was always held at the end of June on the Friday before the school closed. The Frotoft one came a week before that, and the Sourin one was always on the first Friday after the schools opened in August. I was never at a Frotoft picnic until I went to live there but I was allowed to the dance there once I reached the age of sixteen. In those days we had 4 weeks of holidays in July and another 4 weeks in the harvest time.

I was at my first Sourin picnic when I was twelve but there wasn't the magic and excitement that there had been when I was younger. In Frotoft and Sourin the picnics were held at the school but in Wasbister we always went to a field away from the school. Sometimes it was on the braes of Cogar or in Knockha above Innister or at Lee above Langskaill. Everything that was needed was piled on to a horse-drawn cart. Forms for the older folk to sit on, ropes for skipping and starting lines, eggs and spoons and sacks, and of course the food.

We all had to be at the field by two o'clock. On arrival, we were given a delicious cookie with jam and a cup of milk to wash it down. Then the races were run according to age groups. There were adult races as well, such as the cigarette race where the men holding cigarettes stood in a line and the ladies had to run a distance to them and light the cigarettes for them. Then they had to run hand-in-hand back to the starting line. The thread-the-needle race was similar but this time the men did the running holding the thread. When they reached their partners the needles were handed over and the men had to thread them. A tug of war was held with single men on one end and married men on the other. The married men usually won because they were heavier.

About six o'clock we all went back to the school where tea was ready, consisting of bread and jam and curranty buns and biscuits. At that time we had never heard of meat sandwiches. Then the prizes were given out. After that the fiddles appeared and the dancing began. It went on till about 2 o'clock with a break for supper between 10 and 11.

Somehow or other we always got a fine sunny day for our picnic so that we could wear our white ankle socks and plimsolls and bonny cotton frocks.

In my early days at Wasbister school I had two roads to choose from at going home time. I could either take the rough track up between the dykes or I could follow the public road and turn toward home when I reached Grain. One day as I passed Grain I noticed that the barn door was standing open. I glanced in as I passed and saw a large tub standing in the middle of the floor. The place was filled with clouds of steam, but through it I glimpsed the naked form of Ida, the daughter of the house, with her arms stretched above her head. On arriving home I told my mother that I had seen Ida of Grain taking a bath in the barn. My mother laughed, and explained to me that they were killing a pig at Grain that day and what I had seen was the porker suspended over the plowting tub. I still laugh whenever I recall that incident!

Jeannie Gibson, Rousay.

Teachers

Throughout their history, Rousay schools have had comparatively few teachers in charge who were born on the island. Wasbister has had four, the first being Jessie Marwick from Guidal, with Anna May Cooper from the Schoolhouse, Annie F. Craigie from Ivybank, and Lily Miller from Banks, Frotoft coming later. Sarah Craigie from Falquoy was the first Rousay born teacher in Frotoft. The others were Mary Ann Sinclair from Newhouse and Kathleen Gibson (later Harcus) from Hullion. The first Rousay born teacher in Sourin was David Marwick who took up duty in the Society school in 1725. The next one did not appear until 1903 when Jessie Marwick transferred from Wasbister. Sheena Marwick, appointed in 1971, was the third.

The greatly improved ferry services in recent years have made it possible for Rousay residents to travel each day to work on the Mainland, and several now do so. Happily, this also works in reverse, with a young lady from Stromness travelling to Rousay each day to teach in the school there. She must be the first Rousay teacher not to live on the island.

Table 5 — Rousay School Teachers 1843-1960

Frotoft		Sourin			Wasbister	
Year of Appt		Year of Appt	Head	Assistant	Year of Appt	
1854	Sinclair Mackay	1843	Thomas B. Reid		1871	William McKay
1874	Angus McGillvary	1874	James I. Inkster		1875	Roderick McDiarmid
1877	Francis Tocher	1881	John Mpyes		1878	William Cooper
1878	Robert Beattie	1886	Alexander Oswald		1886	Archibald Merilees
1880	Duncan McFadyen	1887	William Wilson		1889	Alexander Horne
1880	Thomas Purdie	1890	William Simpson		1892	John Peace
1886	John Agnew	1894	Alexander McPherson		1899	Mrs. Kate Hadden
1888	Peter L. Muir	1895	David Clouston		1899	Miss Jessie Marwick
1890	Donald McVean	1896	John Carrill		1903	Mrs. McCollie
1894	Mrs. Simpson	1900	Louis McLeod		1904	Miss Martha Wards
1894	Miss Ferguson	1903	Miss Jessie Marwick		1904	Miss B. Norquoy
1896	Mrs Kate Hadden	1905		Miss Cooper	1910	Miss Martha Wards
1899	Jane Sinclair	1906		Miss Woolrage	1913	Miss Magdalene Taylor
1900	Miss Isabella Brass	1907		Miss Moar	1916	Miss Anna May Cooper
1901	David Omand	1908		Miss Malcolmson	1921	Miss Grace Shearer
1901	Miss B. Norquoy	1911	Miss Lydia G. Baikie		1921	Miss Anna F. Craigie
1904	Miss Martha Wards	1925	Miss Mary Rendall		1925	Miss Tina Mathieson
1910	Miss Sarah Craigie	1927		Miss Isacel Craigie	1937	Miss Margt. Sutherland
1914	Miss W. Hourston	1931	Miss I. Craigie	Miss Harper	1941	Mrs. Grace Goar
1918	Miss M. A. Sinclair	1932		Miss Ruby Brown	1943	Mrs. Lily Miller
1934	Miss K. Gibson	1934	John R. Wallace		1960	SCHOOL CLOSED
1947	Miss M. A. Sinclair	1936		Miss Margt. Cooper		
1949	Mrs Isabel Grieve	1938	John Shearer			
1960	SCHOOL CLOSED	1939		Assistant Withdrawn		
		1939	Miss J. G. Mowat			
		1941	Miss Edith McLean			
		1948	Mrs Isabel Grieve			
		1948	Kenneth M. Michie			
		1950	Carl Otto Thomson			
		1953	Mr. J. P. Will			
		1957	Mr G. A. Nelson			

Table 6 — Rousay School Teachers Since 1960

Head Teacher		Assistant	
1960	Mr. G. A. Nelson	1960	Mrs. Lily Miller
1962	Mr. James Merriman	1963	Mrs. K. Harcus
1964	Mr. L. Newall	1966	Mrs. E. B. Firth
1969	Miss S. Williams	1968	Miss S. Williams
1971	Mrs. S. Glendinning		(later Mrs. Grieve)
	(later Mrs. Marwick)	Assistant Withdrawn	
1986	Miss A. Leslie	1972	Mrs Van de Car
	(later Mrs. Mainland)	1986	Mrs. S. Marwick
1990	Mrs S. Marwick (acting)		
1991	Mr. C. Harris	1991	Mrs. S. Marwick
		1993	Miss S. Bain
1994	Mrs. A. Mainland		and
		1994	Mrs. S. Marwick

Appendix
Key to Group Photographs

8. Frotoft School, circa 1913.

Front row L to R: Hugh Sutherland, James Gibson (Hullion), Emmanetta Mainland, David Gibson (Brough), Marie Leonard (Hullion), Kathleen Gibson (Hullion), Harry Logie, Annie Gibson (Hullion), Maggie Ann Craigie (Corse), Tom Sinclair, Annie Leonard (Hullion), Alice Logie (Girlie).
Standing behind: Davidson Harrold, Charles Logie (Lalla), Agnes Robertson (Banks), Isabella Craigie (Corse), James Mainland (Westness), Peggy Sutherland, Jeannie Harrold, Robert Mainland (Westness), Marjorie Gibson (Hullion), Lily Low (Hunclett), James Craigie (Corse), Louise Craigie (Corse), John Mainland (Cott), Edda Mainland (Cott), John Logie (Mount Pleasant), Mary Mainland (Westness), Jeannie Louttit (Evie), Miss Sarah Craigie (Mrs. Costie), John Mainland (Westness), Jim Sinclair (Veira Lodge).

10. Sourin School, 1929/30.

Back row L to R: Miss Mary Rendall, Willie Ferguson, Byng Munro, Alfred Gibson, Robert Seatter, Jeannie Donaldson, Daisy Munro, Jean Clouston, Annabella Gibson, Roy Russell, William Mainland, Leonard Irvine, Miss Isabel Craigie.
Middle row: John Seatter, James Lyon, Annie Craigie, Kathleen Munro, Kathleen Grieve, Mabel Grieve, Nellie Harcus, Chrissie Russell, Kathleen Gibson, Anne Craigie, Isabella Lyon, George Craigie.
Front row: John Grieve, Robert Grieve, Archer Clouston, Edith Gibson, Maggie Ann Munro, Dorothy Mainland, Netta Russell, Ann Lyon, John Harcus, Andy Munro, Angus Harcus.

11. Wasbister School, 1931.

Back row: Miss Tina Mathieson, Stanley Moar, William Marwick, David Wards, Sinclair Craigie, Thomas Donaldson, Thomas Marwick, James Craigie.
Middle row: Jim Sinclair, Clara Donaldson, Agnes Marwick, Netta Sinclair, Jean Marwick, Cathleen Craigie, Clem Donaldson, Anna Marwick, Robert Marwick,
Front row: William Donaldson, Jim Leslie, Donald Marwick.

12. Frotoft School 1936.

Back row L to R: Miss Kathleen Gibson, Ronald Stevenson, Dave Gibson.
Front row: Harry Marwick, John Mainland, Jimmy Pirie.

13. Sourin School, 1936.

Back row: Mr. John Wallace, Angus Harcus, John Grieve, John Seatter, William Mainland, Leonard Irvine, George Craigie, Archer Clouston, Hugh Yorston, Robert Marwick, John Harcus, Miss Ruby Brown.
Middle row back: Dorothy Mainland, Edith Gibson, Sally Linklater, Isobel Pirie, Ann Lyon, Mabel Grieve, Kathy Linklater, Maggie Ann Munro.
Middle row front: Gordon Taylor, George Grieve, Netta Russell, Chrissie Grieve, Dorothy Munro, Thelma Shearer, Robert Lyon, Norman Munro, Robert Munro.
Front row: Andy Munro, Bertie Grieve, Ernest Mainland, Arnold Grieve, Hugh Lyon, James Harcus.

14, Wasbister School, 1939.

Back row: Miss Margaret Sutherland, George Sinclair, David Leslie, Evelyn Clouston, Renie Hourie, Phebe Marwick, Elsie Donaldson, Edwin Moar.
Front row: David Marwick, Cathie Marwick, Edna Clouston, Nettie Marwick, Gertrude Moar, John Marwick.

15. Wasbister School, 1947.

Back row L to R: Freda Grieve, James Marwick, Edna Clouston, Irvine Donaldson, Anita Craigie.
Front row: Mrs. Lily Miller, Margaret Craigie, Margaret Donaldson, Ruth Miller.

16. Frotoft School, 1951.

Back row: Mrs Isabel Grieve, George Craigie, Billy Craigie, Ian Craigie, Bobby Henderson, Mattie Craigie, Tommy Sinclair, Alice Mary Logie.
Front row: Hazel Petrie, Muriel Sinclair, Barbara Henderson. Wilma Gibson, Margaret Gibson, Olive Petrie, Myrtle Petrie, Lilavine Henderson, Mary Gibson, Maisie Drever.

17. Sourin School, 1952/3.

Back row L to R: John Will, George Gillespie, William Grieve, Denis Grieve, Ronald Mainland, Mr. Will.
Middle row: Wilma Mainland, John Inkster, Sinclair Taylor, Tommy Gibson, Marlene Clouston, Kenneth Gillespie, David Will, Sheena Grieve, Muriel Mainland, Leslie Gillespie, Lilian Craigie.
Front row: Ian Grieve, Bob Inkster, Bruce Mainland, Phyllis Clouston.

18. Wasbister School, 1956.

Back row L to R: Sheena Marwick, Harold Grieve, Alison Grieve, James Craigie, Doreen Donaldson, Mrs. Lily Miller.
Front row L to R: Judith Miller, Robert Dickey, Alistair Marwick, William Miller, James Marwick, Marcia Marwick, Phylis Marwick.

19. Rousay School, 1961.

Back row L to R: Leslie Gillespie, John Inkster, Robert Dickie, Kenneth Gillespie, Rona Russell, Doreen Donaldson, Sinclair Taylor, Olive Petrie, Alister Marwick, Jimmy Marwick, Robert Inkster.
Middle row: Julia Gibson, Marcia Marwick, Lillian Craigie, Joyce Lyon, Muriel Mainland, Judy Miller, Doreen Grieve, Phyllis Clouston, Brian Inkster, Bruce Mainland.
Front row: Jeanette Sinclair, Janis Nelson, Harold Trimble, Pat Craigie, Malcolm Lyon, Eric Mainland, Raymond Lyon, Jimmy Clouston, Maureen Gillespie, Byng Munro, Michael Dickie.